GOOD DIRT

Advent, Christmastide & Epiphany

A Devotional for the Spiritual Formation of Families

Lacy Finn Borgo & Ben Barczi

ISBN-10: 1482697459

ISBN-13: 978-1482697452

This book is dedicated to the teachers and staff
of the Renovaré Institute for Spiritual Formation:

Charles Ayers
Howard Baker
Glandion Carney
Richard Foster
Emilie Griffin
Jan Johnson
Keith Matthews
Gary Moon

Regina Moon
John Ortberg
Eduardo Pedreira
James Bryan Smith
Pam Stewart
Chris Webb
Dallas Willard

And with gratitude to our editor, Elane O'Rourke.

CONTENTS

. . . .

Appendices

INTRODUCTION

· ·

Dirt Matters

Pete Collum is my (Lacy's) grandfather and at his very core he is a gardener. Wherever he has lived, he has planted something. When he and my grandmother, Lillian, lived in a dilapidated building that used to be their deli grocery store, surrounded by machine shops and oil field workers, he found tiny patches of dirt and planted watermelons, tomatoes and okra. Armed with a hat that had seen better days, a pocket full of seeds, and a belief in the miracle of growth he stepped into the realm of the Creator and worked. That Permian Basin dirt is full of shale and black gold, but it needs a bit of help if you hope to get squash and tomatoes. He is always puttering around outside, burring scraps, propping up plants, watering, irrigating, and weeding.

It has been said that nature is the first book we read about God. As created beings on a created planet we learn so much from simply looking around a bit.

As a little girl sitting on a paint can in PaPete's garden, I watched him. I saw how the presence of water can change even the look of a plant in a matter of minutes. I saw that if you pull weeds when they are small, their roots are smaller so require less elbow grease to remove. I saw that the row where we buried garden scraps months before had the healthiest plants. I tasted warm watermelon still on the vine, sweetened by the sun.

While listening to Dallas Willard at the Renovaré Institute for Spiritual Formation, this scene came back to me. Spiritual formation has remarkable similarities to garden living and tending. Of course, as parents of young persons and children of God, we live in the garden we tend. The metaphor of the garden can help us enter spiritual formation more fully. And, since we are seasonal creatures born on a seasonal planet, it made perfect sense to me to engage in the Seasons of the Church as part of family spiritual formation. Knowing right away I was in over my head, I enlisted a fellow student, Ben Barczi, for help. He's a spiritual formation pastor who lives the Seasons of the Church. We brainstormed this idea and wrote *Good Dirt* together. It is our desire that our voices are heard in harmony and so many of the narratives are written in first person.

Spiritual Formation: Tending Your Garden

God has given us both the seed of our own souls and the souls of the little ones that live in our homes and leave their gum on the table. Our job is to till, plant, water, and weed, doing what we can to make our family soil rich in the love of God. In the same way that gardens need constant care, so do souls, both little and big ones. This devotional is designed to help you work in the garden of your family throughout your day. It is designed to help you set a daily rhythm of tilling, planting, watering and weeding.

» **Till:** Greet the day with prayer, such as, "Good Morning Master Gardener. We will need your help today. And thanks for the rain." Perhaps praying together at the breakfast table will work for your family, or snuggled together in bed before the day begins.

» **Plant:** Meditate on Scripture, for the good seed of God is his Word. There is nothing better for the little and big souls in families. Read it aloud. Have your newest family reader read, or your oldest, or boldest. What an honor to speak these words of life. If everyone is willing, read it twice. Read it slow. Let it seep in—let it leach the life giving vitamins and minerals into the family. Let it feed these souls.

» **Water:** Reflect. We've got to have water. Water not only hydrates, it also carries vitamins and minerals to where they are needed. Reflection, like water, is a carrier: it carries the truths of Scripture straight to the center of the heart where they can do the most good.

» **Weed:** Examine. If weeds are not pulled in a garden they will choke out all life. That is the harsh truth of gardens and people. Even pre-schoolers can examine their days. They know very well when they have obeyed and when they have not. Just before bedtime is the perfect time to examine the day, to ask the questions: what in my day today was life giving, and what was not? How did I walk in the light today, or not?

Suggested Rhythms for Daily Garden Care:

» **Rhythm #1:**

AM (Breakfast): Till and Plant
Noon: Water
PM (Dinner): Plant and Water
Bedtime: Weed

» **Rhythm #2:**

AM (Breakfast) Till
Noon: Plant
PM (Dinner): Plant, Water
Bedtime: Weed

» **Rhythm #3:**

AM (Breakfast): Till
Noon: Plant, Water
PM (Dinner): Plant, Water

Bedtime: Weed

» **Rhythm #4**

AM (Breakfast): Till, Plant
Noon: Take a pause to thank the Giver of Growth.
PM: (Dinner) Plant, Water
Bedtime: Weed

There are many different combinations that can be used for daily garden care. Between waking up and going to bed, just be sure to till, plant, water, and weed, as a family. As flexible as this can be, it is very helpful to establish a rhythm, the same time to do the same thing day after day. Daily rhythms evoke a sense of security. Rhythms give families a knowing expectation of what is to come.

Spiritual formation has four major elements: your life, spiritual disciplines, Jesus' life, and the Holy Spirit. We have woven these elements into the daily and monthly rhythms. The first element of spiritual formation is **your life.** As a smart-mouthed teen of the '80s I often quipped at friends, "Get a Life." But the truth of the matter is we have a life. We may not love it, and it may not be exactly what we wish, but I've got a life, and you've got a life. You've got a garden. In your garden there is rain, sleet, drought, squirrels, and perhaps on some days too much manure. In your garden you have sprouts; the tiny plants God has given you, the ones that look to you for food and water. The tiny plants that beg to stay up past their bed time, the ones that argue with their sister. The ones that beg for candy in the checkout line, and give away their toys to a friend who has little. You have the shade trees of a good friends, or supportive family. Maybe you've even got a plant or two that would do better in another garden, but you keep it because it's just too hard to change and love rightly. And to keep it real, you've also got weeds; maybe they are sins that seek to choke you or your sprouts.

We are formed by our environment, for good or bad. I spent some of my earliest and best years in my grandparents' old deli in the middle of oil field workers and welding shops. I was formed by this environment. As a result, I learned hospitality: my grandparents welcomed each person who entered their deli. Race or gender had no bearing on how they treated people. I learned responsibility; they gave me jobs to do and the value that came from them depending on my job. I also picked up a colorful vocabulary. I didn't know "shit" was not universally accepted vocabulary until I began attending a Christian School. I did learn fast though.

The second element for spiritual formation is **spiritual practices or disciplines**. These are tools that work life and light into our gardens. Some tools we have used before. They are tried and true. For example, I grew up in a Southern Baptist church, and Southern Baptists read their Bibles and journal. These are good tools to connect us with the Life Changer.

Sometimes we need to change out even our favorite tools. After a while, journaling became a place for me to judge others and whine about my life. So I took a good ten years off journaling. Only recently have I started again, and this time, I only write what I hear God saying to me. The old tool needed retooling, but throw a good tool away? Never. But if the ground has changed, or your soul has had more rain, or even drought, that may call for a new tool.

Spiritual disciplines or practices open the space for God to feed and shape your garden. For example, praying puts you in contact with the Master Gardener. Confession is an exercise in weed pulling. Simplicity keeps us from planting more than our soil can sustain. These habits form us. In this devotional we will engage in many of these life forming habits. We will practice twelve classic practices Richard Foster writes about in his book *Celebration of Discipline*, as well as some others.

The third element for spiritual formation in families is **Jesus' life**. Dallas Willard describes the work of spiritual formation as taking on, bit by bit, Jesus' ideas and images about God, life, and the world, so that they gradually replace our own. We want to be able to look at our everyday life—the dishes, the noisy neighbor, the grubby kids, the mailman, our boss—and be able to see them and live with them in light of the loving, good God that Jesus knew.

The primary place we get instruction and guidance on the with-God life is Jesus. "No one has seen the Father," Jesus' best friend, John, wrote. Now there's a problem—how can we do life with someone no one has ever seen? But John knew the solution, because he snuggled up to him at the Last Supper: "This one-of-a-kind God-Expression, who exists at the very heart of the Father, has made him plain as day." (John 1:18, The Message.)

It is in the one-of-a-kind life and teaching of Jesus that we get the help we need to replace our unhelpful images of God and life with the ones that shaped the mind of Jesus. We watch him talk to God, rejoice in God, weep with God, listen to God, and lead others to God. And, most of all, we see him show God's love: eating with sinners, touching the untouchables, and laying down his life with arms stretched out to embrace the world. That's why in *Good Dirt* we journey with Jesus through the Gospels. In the recorded memories of the disciples, the research of Luke, the reminiscing of Peter handed to Mark, we have an expression of the life of Jesus that takes our breath away—if we will pay attention!

So we need to meditate on and study Jesus' life. Both of those terms get a bad rap, because they sound either mystical or boring. But kids do both naturally. Meditation is just turning over and over an idea, imaginatively, entering it and playing with it and seeing what it means and how it works. Kids meditate on ladybugs and anthills and dog's tails and sand between their fingers. And study—far from being boring work done in a hushed library—is keeping our attention on something so that it becomes part of us. Kids study their favorite super hero, they study mom and dad, they study cartoons and they study their older siblings. ("He's copying me!" Yes, exactly—the child is watching and absorbing mannerisms until they think and act just like the one they've studied.) So studying and meditating aren't as much of a stretch as we'd think, and the Gospels make wonderful material to study Jesus and his one-of-a-kind God-Expression life.

We also get help in journeying with Jesus from the Seasons of the Church. In this devotional we are immersing our lives in the life of Jesus by celebrating the Seasons of the Church. Another way to say it is that we are marking our lives by the life of Jesus. The Christian Church began formally celebrating Easter as early as 325AD, and even before that Israel had seasons of fasting and feasting to mark their story with God throughout the ages. There is a great cloud of witnesses that have gone before us.

The seasons follow a pattern of preparation, celebration, and then living out what we have prepared for and celebrated. In Advent we prepare for God with us, at Christmastide we celebrate God with us, and during Epiphany we step into a life with God. In Lent we prepare for our own death and the death of Jesus, at Eastertide we celebrate that he died, is risen and us with him, and during Pentecost and Kingdomtide we live out his resurrection and ours. We are meant to live seasonally. Who can feast all the time without becoming a glutton? Who can fast or mourn all the time without losing their mind? When our days lose the gift of thankfulness and celebration we become a depressed and dying people. As the physical seasons set the rhythm of the earth, so the church season can set our rhythm to the rhythm of Christ.

There are seven main seasons of the church. The great diversity of our Christian traditions means that some seasons are named slightly differently and some dates are variable, but this is the overall, middle of the road, happy medium, church calendar.

Seasons of the Church

» **Advent:** Four weeks. Color: Royal Blue

» **Christmastide:** Twelve days, until the eve of Epiphany on January 5. Color: White

» **Epiphany:** Eight weeks, give or take a few weeks depending on when Easter falls; plus a little at the beginning and a little at the end to get us to Ash Wednesday for Lent. Color: Green

» **Lent:** Five weeks, plus a little at the beginning and a full week of Holy Week. Color: Purple

» **Eastertide:** Seven weeks up to Trinity Sunday. Color: White

» **Pentecost:** One week, which is included in the first week of Kingdomtide. Color: Red

» **Kingdomtide:** Twenty-Eight weeks, give or take a few weeks depending on when Easter falls. Color: Green

Do all these dates sound confusing? No worries, we put a calendar of specific dates at the end of the book. In time these seasons will become second nature.

How to Make a Seasons of the Church Calendar

First, a confession. The first three times I made one of these it was a disaster, mostly because I'm an adult. In my first attempt, I couldn't make myself label the seasons counter-clockwise. The calendar moves counterclockwise to remind us that we live countercultural to the world and its systems of destruction and death. However, in my forty years on this planet, I have learned that everything moves clockwise; going against the grain requires more thinking than I can summon. Funny thing though, my seven year old and ten year old pulled it off. "It's easy, Mom," they said. Likely story. In my second attempt, I spelled Epiphany wrong, in permanent marker. My Southern Baptist roots betray me. Who ever heard of Epiphany in the first place? And for my final attempt, I couldn't get the dashes evenly spaced to mark the weeks. There were rulers, protractors, and a host of other instruments I hadn't used since high school geometry. Once again counseled by people not even of driving age, I realized I was letting this calendar use me. Got it. So I stepped back and let the kids make it. It's great and it's attached to our fridge.

Materials: poster board, pencils, permanent markers, rulers (only one and no more tools) crayons, 1 brass brad

1. This calendar will look very much like an analog clock. Cut a large circle (as large as you want your calendar to be) out of the poster board.

2. Divide the calendar into seven sections, like a pie graph. Take a look at the seasons listed above, estimate that, for example Kingdomtide will need the most space because it has the most weeks. Pentecost and Christmastide will have tiny spaces. Remember: the seasons go in counter-clockwise order. For example: make a space for Advent, then move to the left for Christmastide, etc. If you get stuck ask your kid for help.

3. Within each season make "dashes," like the five minute marks on an analog clock, to represent the weeks contained in each season.

4. Write the name of the season on its space. Fill in the season space with its color, (see the list above.)

5. Cut out an arrow from the poster board. Use the brass brad to attach it to the middle of the calendar.

Optional Additions: put a star on Christmastide, and a Cross on the first week of Eastertide. Invite or encourage your children to research the history and tradition of the seasons and write a list of their symbols in their space. Decorate the house with these symbols when their season comes around. A friend of mine has wind chimes hanging over her kitchen bar, and changes the items on the chime as the seasons change. We change the items on our mantle. All of this is not to make us consumers; in fact it's more fun to make some of these items. Like the icons used in the Orthodox Christian tradition, they are open windows into the life of Jesus. They remind us that we mark our lives by his life.

The fourth element for spiritual formation in families is the **Holy Spirit**. We can prepare the dirt, we can water and weed, but we don't make things grow. We have no control over sun, rain or wind. We aren't even in charge of the seed we are given: we do not choose our talents and inclinations. The Holy Spirit gives the seed. The Holy Spirit makes things grow. We do not control the outcomes, and it's a good thing: having control is dangerous for us. Getting just what we want and hope can make us hell to live around. Having complete control leads us to cast judgment on others. Even thinking we should have control can make us a mess. Think of the parents of children who have struggled or self-destructed? Parents who think they are in control beat themselves up for doing it wrong. They carry the crushing burdens of "should have", "would have" and "could have." How wonderful that we have the Holy Spirit working on our behalf. We learn to do our part and trust the Holy Spirit for the rest.

Everybody's Got Parts

In a garden, plants have parts. And those parts have different jobs and have different needs. People have parts too. The most obvious part we have is our body.

We were only one song into Sunday morning when Julie began to lead them in. All seven preschoolers followed dutifully behind our children's director to the front row. The switch to modern worship music hasn't been easy for most of the church. The hymns are the songs of their faith, their struggles, but graciously, they sing. They don't clap, but they do sing. And so did the preschoolers. They belted out those tunes like they had sung them all their lives. First they worshiped with their mouths. Then a few began to sway, they started clapping their hands, and a few even let loose a full-body jig. As someone who is with children on a regular basis this was no surprise to me. I know they can't hide joy in their bodies. But I was surprised at how their transparency spread through the church. While the congregation watched the children, who frankly couldn't be ignored, folks began to smile, and then clap, and even dare I say it, sway. "Is this how the children will lead us?" I thought. They will lead us to worship God with our whole selves.

Children, like adults, have parts. Children have a body, a mind, a spirit, a soul, and a village. Dallas Willard in *Renovation of the Heart* calls "village" a social context.[1] This refers to the folks that influence us as well as the ones we influence. This village does shape us. Jesus mentions each of these parts as he gives us the For Dummies version of the Ten Commandments, "Love the Lord you God with all your heart [spirit], and with all your soul [soul] and with all your mind, [mind], with all your strength [body]…, and love your neighbor [village or social context] as yourself." (Mark 12:30-31) When we talk about spiritual formation we are talking about all these parts being invited into relationship with God. All of these parts come to live in the kingdom of God.

Our children's bodies which we lovingly wash and feed are created by God and created like all their other parts to be in relationship with him. As a born Southern Baptist, who is currently Nazarene, but loves everything Catholic, I have to say that the best part of the twelve days of Christmastide is meditating on the Incarnation. God himself enters creation in a human body, a real human body. The Gnostics and the church Fathers went round and round over this. Did Jesus have a real human body, you know, one that got the flu and threw up, one that had body odor, one that danced when he felt joy, one that wept when he felt sadness? Our Church Fathers fought the good fight to say that, yes, he had and still does have a real body. For us, the incarnation, Jesus in a real human body, means that our bodies are redeemable. God's intention for bodies is goodness. He declares it so in Genesis 1, and who am I to contradict that?

Children cannot hide the condition of their spirit, mind or emotion behind their bodies. Adults can, but children simply cannot pull it off. This is a major advantage for children as we think about how they live their lives with Jesus. When they are sad, sadness leaks out of their eyes; it is shown in their bodies. Adults, on the other hand, have been taught when these emotions are appropriate and when they are not, and we are often trained to deny even having these emotions.

Equally so, children can't hide their thoughts. During sharing time in thousands of elementary schools across America, children are sharing what they are thinking about. Mostly what they have to say is not even loosely related to the topic at hand, but it's on their mind and they have a desire to tell someone.

---

1 For a full and frankly fantastic teaching on the parts of the person and how they are formed into Christlikeness check out *Renovation of the Heart* by Dallas Willard.

The desire to share comes from the divinely inspired, very human, desire to be known—for the hidden parts of us to be known and accepted by another. Children in healthy environments have no inclination that hidden parts should stay hidden or that any thought they have wouldn't be welcomed by any hearers.

Rightly ordered the spirit is the command center of the person. "Out of the heart the mouth speaks," the Scriptures remind us. Jesus refers to it in his simple version of the commandments. "Love the Lord your God with all your heart and soul." However our spirit is formed so goes the rest of the person. Interestingly enough educational sciences are discovering that we are formed by experiences more than we are formed by formal teaching. Churches over the last hundred or so years have invested truck loads of resources in education of children and I think if we look back we might question the results. At least in the last twenty years we have seen a mass exit of young people from the church. Could one of the reasons be that formal teaching does not actually hold the weight in formation that experience does? Could it be that the experiences of formation offered by the secular world outweighed the formal teaching of Christian education?

The key to the power in experience over formal teaching lies in our wiring. We are created to take in information through our five senses, engaging all the parts of our person. What the body experiences is taken into the spirit, and like capillary action moves to all our other parts and formation happens. Living a life with God is not confined to an intellectual understanding. All the parts of the person live a life with God. Everything. He came to redeem it all. That's the good news. We get a whole, not partial, salvation.

Seasonal Fun

The seasonal fun section contains opportunities to mark our lives by the life of Jesus. In this section there are many activities, crafts, celebrations, suggestions, songs, harebrained ideas, and general chances for fun. Please, do not set out to do them all. Do not. You will make yourself and your family crazy. Instead, during each season choose a few, the ones that are suited to where you are in your family, for example toddlers versus teenagers. Next year choose some that you didn't do the previous year.

Marking your life by the life of Jesus for one year will change you for sure, but imagine with me the difference it will make marking it each year for the rest of your life on earth. Imagine. Imagine the difference it will make in the lives of your children as you bring them into the knowledge and relationship with Jesus first through observation and participation in the rituals of the season and then when they are old enough reading through the gospels.

Seasonal Fun is where we live out in our bodies the marking of our lives by Jesus' life. For example, the celebration of Eastertide has its chance to work resurrection into our minds through bodies as we have a mini-celebration every Sunday during the seven weeks of the season.

Family Structures

In this devotional we reference moms and dads and children. But rest assured, if your family structure doesn't look like this, this is still for you! Today's family structures are varied and those structures too are included in Jesus' invitation to the kingdom. Our intimate communities often include friends, and extended family members. From my point of view this is wonderful. When we use the word "family" in this devotional we are including those in your intimate community, those living and eating with you.

Family Listening

As a people we're pretty good about talking, and telling. We've got stories to tell and opinions to convey. However, part of the relationship process with each other and with God is listening. In this devotional we will encourage you to practice listening. Good listening, complete with eye contact, affirmations, and a zippered lip. Every day you will be challenged to listen to God, and to discern with one another his voice and message. We often think of hearing from God as an-other worldly, only-when-smoke-is-involved matter, but that couldn't be farther from the truth. Listening to God, like listening to others, is a product of experience. You know your mother's voice because you have heard it over and over again. When we hear a voice we think is God's we check it against 1 Corinthians 13. Was the voice patient and kind? How about gentle and generous? If so that was God and we fix that experience in our souls. Each additional experience we have with God's voice builds our confidence. After a while it won't be long before we don't even have to look we know it was God who spoke, because we've heard him before.[2]

And What about the Littlest People?

This is a family rhythm, and because families can range in ages, we've aimed at the middle. Every aspect—Till, Plant, Water and Weed—can be "rounded" up or down. "Rounding" up is rarely a problem, but what about the littlest members of our family? How does this nurture the preschool people?

These little interactive sponges have all senses on go! The real value of ritual, which involves so many of the senses, is spent on the little ones. Each night during Advent as the candles are lit, their minds are drinking in that 'light dispels darkness' and 'the One who is celebrated is the light.' The regularity of ritual teaches far more than wordy explanations. The Seasonal Fun section is the main teaching tool for small children. In living the seasons and reading the scriptures year after year, an essential foundation is being built on the Rock. They are listening when the scriptures are being read. Furthermore, they understand far more than we realize. It is not that we, the knowing adults, have to introduce them to God. They very recently were knitted together in their mother's womb. They know the Knitter. However, at their developmental stage they lack the language to express what they know. It is, nevertheless, up to us, their parents, to teach them the language, and to teach them what a relationship with God looks like on this earth.

---

2 Dallas Willard's book *Hearing God: Developing a Conversational Relationship with God,* has been instrumental in deepening our knowledge and practice of hearing and discerning the voice of God.

ADVENT

. . . .

I (Lacy) hear the laments of parents. I am a lamenting parent. Christmas is too much about the stuff. The stuff begins to clog up the supermarket aisles as early as September. My kids are bombarded by ads trying to get them, to get me, to want to buy them their heart's desire of shiny junk. As a Christian I want to celebrate the birth of Jesus in a way that honors him and follows in his ways. Advent is four weeks of preparation for the King of Creation. When we put it that way it almost seems that four weeks isn't long enough. Blue is the color for the season, specifically Royal Blue as my eldest daughter reminds me, because Jesus is the King. I admit sometimes I forget that. With all the sale ads and the meals to prepare and the ever present Christmas music, I can hardly think, I can hardly remember. Advent is preparation, it's remembering that Royal Blue is for a Royal King. With all the distraction that is modern life, plus the added distraction of Christmas, we need ways to remember.

Several years ago at Ridgeland Community Church some saintly ladies taught me the importance of Advent. They limped my non-crafty self through the process of making an Advent wreath. They taught me the significance of preparation for the Christ Child. I am forever grateful. Through the practice of Advent I learned to lean in and celebrate this blessed holiday. During those first few years of practicing Advent it was just my husband and I, and surprisingly we never fought over who got to blow out the candles. Now, my children take turns to see who gets to blow candle wax all over the table. Advent is a staple in our home. It is a practice that grounds us to the truths of Jesus.

Advent Wreaths

Traditional Advent wreaths have four candles to represent the four weeks of Advent, three purple candles and one pink. The wreath itself is usually made of evergreen branches to represent everlasting life in Jesus. The circle of the Advent wreath signifies God, who has no beginning and no end. Some modern wreaths have a single white candle, lit on Christmas Eve, in the middle that reminds us that Christ is the focus. Our family has remade some of the Advent traditions. I'm not a big fan of pastels, so each November, I let the kids choose new candles in anticipation of the coming of Advent. Instead of the birth order deciding who lights the candles, we simply take turns.

A good time to celebrate Advent is during the dinner time meal. Unfortunately, for us, it doesn't work so well. My husband works shift work, and many times he's not home during dinner. So we may celebrate at breakfast, lunch, dinner, or even stop in the middle of the afternoon. If he can't make it we proceed without him, praying for him in his work.

We begin our celebration by lighting the candle(s) for the corresponding week. At that point you can follow the family rhythm of Till, Plant, Water, and Weed. Wherever you are in the rhythm, pick up and go. Some families may Till and Plant in the morning, then Water and Weed during dinner. Other families may Till, Plant, Water and Weed after the candle(s) are lit. (See page 2 for a reminder of these themes.)

Boisterous Singing?

Singing is a product of celebration and worship. Humans instinctively sing when we're happy and often we sing when we are in "awe" of something or someone. Think of all the love songs in this world. Advent is both a raucous celebration and a reason to worship—to sing our love songs to God. If you are not much of a singer you may be inclined to skip this section; please don't. Give it a week, sing with all you have, and see if your body, mind and spirit don't follow. Second, if you are celebrating Advent with your children, they will love it and in fact they need it. A great way to learn is through song, by repetition. For that reason we encourage you to sing the same song each day for one week. By the end of the week you may be sick of it, but your children will have learned it, and hidden those words of love, joy, celebration, and worship in their hearts.

Fasting

Fasting during the Holiday Season? Yes! Fasting has been used as a tool for thousands of years to help us listen. By turning off other things we open our hearts and minds to God who longs to whisper his great love to those who will listen. There are many ways and many things that we can fast to prepare for the Royal Baby.

>   » This time of year strikes fear in the minds of all parents who have the foresight to consider all the sugar their children are about to ingest. As a family, save all sweets for Sunday. Sundays are traditionally celebration days, even during a time of fasting. Every Sunday we celebrate the resurrection—and what better way to "taste and see that the Lord is good," than by saving the sweets for Sunday? Remember we are moving "counter-clockwise" to our culture. Here in the season of Advent, we actively wait.

>   » Fast from media, when all family members are together. Evenings are usually the best time for most families. You can replace usual TV time with a Seasonal Fun activity, a family game, or read together. Try *The Story of the Other Wise Man*.[3]

>   » Two Saturdays during Advent eat rice and beans only. Breakfast, lunch and dinner. Discuss what it must be like to have this every day. Decide as a family on a charity you would like to work with during the Holidays.

>   » Give up your gifts. Fast from giving gifts to each other this year. Instead, use the money to buy gifts for a family in your community who has very little. Plan a covert operation to drop off the gifts without being caught. Spend all four weeks of Advent planning.

---

3 Henry Van Dyke, *The Story of the Other Wise Man*. Paraclete Press. 2008.

The Jesse Tree

Isaiah 11:1 says, "A shoot will spring forth from the stump of Jesse, and a branch out of his roots." The Jesse tree is a visual history of 4,000 years of God's faithfulness. Since Advent is the beginning of our church year, it is fitting that we begin with the firm foundation of the human experience of a life with God. Each day will have a reading of Scripture, and a symbol that can be hung on your Jesse Tree. You'll need a few things:

» The Actual Tree: You need a tree. Since Isaiah 11:1 says "stump, and branch," that's what we use. Just before Advent we take a stroll through our backyard/woods and choose four branches, each a bit longer than the last. None of your branches should be more than 18 inches long. Take your longest branch and attach the smaller branches perpendicular to the larger one. We use string. Then stand up your tree. In the past, we have stuck our branch in a pot of dirt, or attached a wad of play dough to the bottom, or used a block of wood into the middle of which we burrowed a hole. Don't see this as a burden, but instead get the whole family involved in problem solving the "how to make our Jesse Tree stand up" project. You may just find you have a budding engineer in your home. (If your family puts up your Christmas tree early, you can also hang your symbols on it.)

» Symbols: The symbols for the Jesse Tree can be found in many places on the internet, just "Google" "Jesse Tree." They can be printed out, hand colored or embellished and then hung. You can also invite your people to draw the symbol, or use dough to create it. We have done both.

» Time: Warning—this is not a jiffy-quick devotional to ease Christian parental guilt. A life with God is the foundation of the lives of those who call themselves "friends of God." This tool requires time. It will yield great results in the soul-soil of all who participate, but as with anything worthwhile, it will take sacrifice. The time invested is time well spent. The Jesse Tree will take about an hour a day. We suggest doing it at night, maybe after dinner. The ritual is simple. Read the scriptures, (as it is only a short reading fill in any gaps in your own words—this is the part my children think is the most fun. We like to talk about the lives of those who have walked with God before us) then create and hang the symbol on your tree.

Just Say Slow

This time of year is the busiest. Gifts to buy, parties to attend, food to make, and that is in addition to work, school and kids. On our continent, creation has taken its cues from the earth and is slowing down. During Advent the first signs of winter come. The trees are brown, animals are hibernating, and the sun sets earlier. There is more dark than light. Dark gives the signal to our bodies—slow down, reflect, and savor. It never makes sense to go against God's already established rhythm.

Advent is waiting time, where the air is literally pregnant with the presence of God. Like all pregnancies, too much stress and strain is not good for growing. So slow down, make the space each day to watch and wait as your family grows with Mary's belly, ripe with the Christ child. I encourage you to change gears this year. Get off the holiday treadmill, and savor these quiet moments of Advent. Say "No, thanks," to a few invitations and responsibilities, "I've got a baby to wait for."

ADVENT, WEEK 1

....

Seasonal Fun

The color of Advent has traditionally been purple. Our liturgical church family members wear purple vestments. Purple is the color of royalty; our King, who we wait for this season, is of royal blood. However, there have been recent changes to this tradition and some folks are leaning toward blue. The season of Lent is also purple and in a nod to simplicity many have changed the color of Advent to blue. For our purposes, go with what your own church family chooses, or pick the one you like the best. In *Good Dirt* we have chosen blue to highlight the contrast between the season of Lent and the season of Advent.

» Fun things to do with color: purchase or make special blue bowls or napkins/table cloth to use during Advent. Invite children to create paintings of what Advent is all about using only shades of blue. Display their art in a prominent place. Purchase blueberry soda, make blueberry muffins, put a few drops of blue food color in mac n cheese. These are just suggestions; ask your kids to help you think of ways to decorate in blue. Have fun.

» Advent Wreath: Take the family to a candle store to pick out candles for your Advent wreath. You can choose the traditional (three purple and one pink) or go crazy let the kids pick out their favorite colors. Let the children help set up the wreath. Invite the oldest child to light the first candle each night this week.

» Make an Advent Calendar: Take 24 baby socks and clothespin them to a long piece of yarn. Using a permanent marker write the numbers 1-24, one for each sock. Fill each sock with a note, or a package of Smarties for the children to share. Note ideas: a note of praise for specific children and a specific deed, a special event for that day (ex: making cookies for the Pastor), a special privilege.

» Nativity: Set out a Nativity set, but only put out the barn. Scatter the other pieces of the scene around the house. Explain to the children that the season of Advent is the season of waiting. We're waiting for the Christ Child to come. Tell the children that each day we will move the pieces a little closer to the barn. (Of course the animals will need to get there first.)

» Boisterous Song: *O Come, O Come Emmanuel.* Sing during Advent time. If you do not know the words to this song, check out your church hymnal. If your church does not have a hymnal, "Google" the title.

» Jesse Tree: If your family is doing the Jesse Tree, here are the readings for Week One:

  » Day 1—Scripture: Isaiah 11:1-10; Symbol: The Tree

  » Day 2—Scripture: Genesis: 1:24-28; Symbol: Three Circles Interconnected

  » Day 3—Scripture: Genesis 2:4-3:24; Symbol: An Apple

  » Day 4—Scripture: Genesis 6:11-22, 8:6-12; Symbol: Rainbow

  » Day 5—Scripture: Genesis 12:1-7, 13:2-18; Symbol: Stars

  » Day 6—Scripture: Genesis 22:1-19; Symbol: Ram

  » Day 7—Scripture: Genesis 27:41-28:22; Symbol: Ladder

First Sunday of Advent

Till: Powerful God, help us be on the lookout for you today! Give us watchful eyes so we can be with you today and, when Jesus returns, live with him forever.

Plant: Matthew 25:1-13

Water:

> » Play it: Re-enact the story as a short drama. Allow one child to be the 'director' (take turns!). Help the kids see the events of the story.

> » Apply it: Jesus tells this story to remind us that we are waiting for him. We can be on the lookout for him, expecting him to help us in big and small ways each day. Where can you be on the lookout for Jesus today?

Weed: How were you able to be on the lookout for God today? What is one way you could remember Jesus' love for you tomorrow?

Monday

Till: Jesus, we know God sent you to teach and help us! Please be with us today in everything we do.

Plant: Luke 20:1-8

Water:

> » Enter it: Imagine your teacher asks you to tell the other students in your class to clean up the games they are playing. But when you tell them, they say, "Who sent you? I don't have to listen to you!" (That's just how the leaders were treating Jesus!) How would you feel? How do you think your teacher would feel?

> » Apply it: Jesus knew the leaders were going to pretend not to know the answer to his question, because they just didn't want to follow Jesus.

They didn't want to love people like He taught. What is one way Jesus might want to teach you to love better today?

Weed: Share one way you were loving today—to parents, brothers and sisters, or friends. What was one time you didn't want to listen today? Why not?

Tuesday

Till: Jesus, you are the Son of God! Be with us today and help us to work, play and live with you.

Plant: Luke 20:9-18

Water:

>> Play it! Re-enact the story as a short drama. Allow one child to be the 'director'(take turns). Help the kids see the events of the story.

>> Apply it: God sent his son Jesus, but lots of people didn't want to accept him—they wanted to do things their own way. What is one way you can welcome Jesus into your day today?

Weed: Were you able to welcome Jesus today like you planned? Was it easy, or hard? How could you welcome Jesus tomorrow?

Wednesday

Till: God, you made each one of us special, just for you! Help us remember your love today.

Plant: Luke 20:19-26

Water:

» Create it: Help kids make some masking-tape labels or signs that say "Caesar's" and some that say, "God's." Have them first stick some "Caesar's" labels on material things—money, a toy, the house, etc. (Make sure the labels will come off easily first.) Then have them stick the "God's" label on themselves, each other, and even on you! Wear your "God's" label all day long.

Weed: When did you remember God today? How did it make you feel to remember God loves you? Was there a time you forgot you were loved by God, and acted badly? How could you remember you are God's in that situation tomorrow?

Thursday

Till: God, we're made to live with you forever! Just one day close to you would be even better than thousands of years anywhere else. Help us to start living with you today.

Plant: Luke 20:27-40

Water:

» Create it: Jesus tells us that everyone who trusts him will live forever with God! Draw a picture of what you imagine it will be like to live with God. In your picture, include some of your favorite people from the Bible—like Abraham, or Noah, or David, or Mary—because they will be there too.

» Apply it: In today's story, the Sadducees try to stump Jesus with a story about a woman who has many husbands. They can't imagine that anything would be more important in heaven than being with loved ones—but Jesus says that being with God is far better. What are some things that you can't imagine being without? Today, consider that being with God is even more of a treasure than these good things.

Weed: Name some of the good things God generously gave you today. Try to name 10 blessings. Pick one good thing that you are looking forward to tomorrow. How could this blessing remind you that God is better than anything else?

Friday
......

Till: Jesus, teach me to give you everything! Thank you for being excited about my small acts of love and kindness.

Plant: Luke 20:41-21:4

Water:

> » Play it! Have kids play-act the two different characters in this story— first, those who like being noticed in giving a lot (Perhaps the kids hold up an "applause" sign as they put a dollar in a jar?), and second, the woman who gives just two pennies, even though it's all she has.

> » Apply it: Jesus taught that it's not how big or important our good deeds seem to others that matters, but whether we give what we have to give—that's real extravagance! Help each child name some ways they can share and love right now that might not seem like a big deal, but please God very much.

Weed: What was one small thing you did today to show love? Tomorrow, how would you like to share and love even more than today?

Saturday
....

Till: Jesus, even when things are scary, you take care of us! Thank you! Help us stick close to you today.

Plant: Luke 21:5-19

Water:

» Create it: Jesus names a lot of scary things in today's reading—but then says that, through it all, he is with us. Draw a picture, or make a Silly Putty sculpture, that shows Jesus with you. (Silly Putty is super cheap and great to use with kids. It keeps their hands busy while engaging their mind. Adults love it, too.)

» Enter it: Name a time when you are afraid. How does it make you feel to know that Jesus is with you, even when you are afraid?

» Apply it: When things get scary, it's hard to remember Jesus is with us. Choose an object—a tiny stuffed animal, or a picture of Jesus (or something more symbolic for older kids, like a cross or rock)—that you could hold onto when you are frightened, to remind you Jesus is with you. (Let older children carry it today. Younger kids might have it by the bed.)

Weed: How did it make you feel to have your object with you today? Did it help? (Or, for younger kids, how do you feel knowing Jesus will be with you all night tonight?) Name one scary thing that you can trust Jesus to help you with tomorrow.

ADVENT, WEEK 2

....

Seasonal Fun:

» Advent Wreath: Each night this week light two Advent candles. During the reading give each child and adult an "egg" of Silly Putty invite them to make an object that most represents how they are feeling about Jesus right now.

» Alleluia List: This time of year is full of lists. Christmas Gift Lists, Grocery Lists, Things to Do Lists—even Santa's makin' a list, and I'm told he's checking it twice. This year make a new list. The most effective way of teaching our children about the goodness of God is by counting our blessings. Augustine said to be an "Alleluia from head to toe." Beginning this week, start an Alleluia List. Take newsprint or long butcher paper, every evening before going to bed invite all members of the family to rattle off things that they are thankful for. Make a long list. The only rule is that nothing can be listed twice. Hang the list where it can be seen and added to nightly.

» Nativity: Each day invite the children to move the Nativity pieces closer to the barn.

» If you have preschool children, help them make a few Christmas Cards out of cardstock. Cutting up last year's Christmas cards and gluing the pictures to new ones can be fun. Help them write Merry Christmas. Take the cards to a nursing home and give them away. The relationship between children and the elderly is reciprocal, good for everyone.

The elderly love children and exposing children to the elderly help the children not to be afraid. Tell the children before you go that the elderly might want to hold hands. Tell them that older folks are not scary, their bodies are just old and some parts don't work anymore. But God still loves them and so do we. Use this opportunity to teach the compassion of Jesus. In the kingdom of God there are no throw-away people. Always stay with your child, and set the example of loving others. Some children love to perform and sing. Here is a place they can do just that, while serving Jesus.

» Boisterous Song: *O Come All Ye Faithful*. Sing during Advent time. If you do not know the words to this song, check out your church hymnal. If your church does not have a hymnal, "Google" the title.

» Jesse Tree: If your family is doing the Jesse Tree, here are the readings for Week Two:

   » Day 1—Scripture: Genesis 37:1-36; Symbol: Coat

   » Day 2—Scripture: Exodus 2:1- 4:20; Symbol: Burning Bush

   » Day 3—Scripture: Exodus 19:1-20:20; Symbol: 10 Commandments

   » Day 4—Scripture: Joshua 1:1-11, 6:1-20; Symbol: Ram's Horn Trumpet

   » Day 5—Scripture: 1 Samuel 3:1-21; Symbol: Lamp

   » Day 6—Scripture: 1 Samuel 16:14-23; Symbol: Harp

   » Day 7—Scripture: Psalm 23; Symbol: Shepherd's Staff

Second Sunday of Advent

Till: God, you are a good King! In your kingdom there is room for loud rejoicing and room for quiet waiting. In your kingdom everyone has an important part to play. In your kingdom, we are safe! Let your kingdom come!

Plant: Luke 7:28-35

Water:

» Enter it: When John the Baptist came, lots of people didn't like how he lived in the desert and fasted and prayed all the time—too hard! When Jesus came, lots of people didn't like how he loved and ate with everyone, good and bad, and had fun and rejoiced with people— too easy! How do you think this made God feel?

» Apply it: John taught people that sometimes we need to be serious about changing the way we live, to get ready for God. Jesus taught that sometimes we need to rejoice because God loves us even now. And both were right! What is one thing you can change today? What is one thing you can rejoice in today? (Help your younger children make a plan that you can do with them.)

Weed: What did you change today? How did that change your day? When did you rejoice today? How did that change your day?

Monday
· · · · · · · ·

Till: Jesus, you are coming back to make everything right! So even in the darkest, scariest time, we can hold our heads high in hope. Come, Lord Jesus! Help us hope in you today.

Plant: Luke 21:20–28

Water:

» Play it: In today's reading, Jesus is giving us a picture of what it will be like when he returns—and it's a frantic, explosive image! Play this game—invite the children to be as chaotic, frantic, wild as they like (create a safe, controlled space for this! Are there pillows they can throw, etc?), for a minute, and then be completely silent for a minute. Tell them when you lift your hands, they can go wild, but when you lower them they have to stay completely still. (This will probably take a few rounds, but make it a challenge—how still can they be?) After they have been really still, congratulate them! Then read the passage again. (This exercise is borrowed from Kathleen Norris' book *Amazing Grace*.)

» Enter it: During the "chaos" time, how did you feel? What is an image that captures it? Describe it, or draw it. (Older kids can write about it.) Now, describe the silence. How did that feel? What image captures stillness? Describe it, or draw it.

» Apply it: Jesus teaches us that no matter how crazy or scary things get, we should look for him to be with us—both now, and when He comes again. Is there anything scary today that you can do with Jesus?

Weed: What was hard, or scary today? Were you able to remember that Jesus was with you? How can you remember that Jesus is with you tomorrow?

Tuesday

Till: Jesus, help us be alert! Help us be ready! You show up every day, and you are coming for us some day. Keep us watchful!

Plant: Luke 21:29-38

Water:

» Play it: Play a game of "reflex" to help kids get the idea of being alert and ready: have the child hold their hands out; gently and quickly try to touch one of their hands before they can take it away. You can have kids play this together as long as they can control how hard they touch and won't hurt each other.

» Create it: If there are autumn leaves still on any trees or on the ground, have kids collect them. Put them on the fridge (or someplace visible) as reminders—just as we can tell that the season is changing, we should be on the lookout for where Jesus is showing up in our lives, and for his return.

Weed: Where and when did you think about God today? Advent is all about waiting for God, expecting him. How can you be on the lookout for his love and help tomorrow?

Wednesday

Till: Jesus, you help us every time we forget you. You forgive us for every time we disobey you. Thank you! Help us return to you today, because you love us.

Plant: John 7:53-8:11

Water:

» Apply it: Jesus sets an example for how we should treat others who are caught doing something wrong: we can forgive and help them, because we also need help and forgiveness. Can you think of a time when someone frustrated or disappointed you? What would it look like to forgive them?

» Enter it: (For younger kids you may want to encourage them to draw or describe aloud what they imagine as you go along. Older kids can do this quietly. With very young kids you might just have them imagine Jesus hugging them and describe that.) Imagine that you are brought before Jesus, with someone pointing out a bad thing you have done. (Invite older kids to think of a specific sin.) How do you feel? What is the look on Jesus' face? (Give kids a moment to picture this.) Now you hear Jesus say, "I forgive you. You don't need to be afraid!" Picture Jesus' face now. How does he seem to you? (Pause and allow kids to picture this.) Now Jesus gives you a big hug, and says, "You don't have to do that harmful thing anymore. You are free! Go and enjoy a good life!" How do you feel? Look up at his face—how does he look at you?

» Optional activity: Have kids create a "storyboard" drawing of each scene in this vivid story. Make a picture of: 1) The leaders throwing the woman on the ground before Jesus. 2) Jesus writing in the dirt, saying

"The sinless one can throw the first stone." 3) The leaders confused and walking away. 4) Jesus talking kindly to the woman.

Weed: Think back over your day. Where did you remember that Jesus loves you? How did you feel then? When did you disobey? Or forget God's love? (You may want to have younger children say this out loud, but have older children consider this quietly.) Return to the image of Jesus hugging you and saying, "You don't have to do that anymore! You're free!" Hold on to that picture as you go to sleep tonight.

Thursday

Till: Jesus, you are the Lamb of God, who died because you love us! You have mercy on us. Jesus, you are the Lamb of God, who died because you love us! Help us to feel restful and happy in your love.

Plant: Luke 22:1-13

Water:

> » Enter it: In today's reading, we are approaching the time when Jesus is betrayed, arrested, and crucified. Judas goes behind Jesus' back and arranges with the leaders to hand Jesus over to them. Have you ever had someone you trusted let you down? Can you describe how you think Jesus felt?

> » Apply it: The disciples and Jesus are about to celebrate an important meal to remember what God had done for them when he set the Israelites free from slavery. Let's remember some things God has done for us: can you name five good things we can thank God for today?

> » Optional activity: In today's and tomorrow's readings, Jesus and his disciples celebrate the Passover, and Jesus gives us Communion to remember him. The tangible symbols of the bread and the cup can be very helpful for kids to grasp Jesus' sacrifice. Here are a few ideas to help kids engage Communion:

Today, pour a glass of grape juice and break a piece of bread with your kids, and place them in a prominent place (by your Advent wreath, for instance). Explain what the elements mean and let their presence be a reminder.

Get some grapes or grape-vines and some wheat-like grain and make a wreath or add these to your advent wreath arrangement.

Help the kids to understand the "Lamb of God" by reading the Exodus story, in Exodus 12:1-28. Make a lamb (glue cotton balls to a paper sheep body) and place the lamb somewhere prominent, like your advent wreath or on your Christmas tree.

Weed: Tonight, as kids go to bed, place in their room, near their bed, some symbol—a cross, a lion, a dove, a crown, a shepherd's staff, etc. Ask, "What does this symbol tell us about who God is?"

Friday
......

Till: Jesus, you are our King—but you love us so much that you serve us! Help us to learn to love others like you love us. Help us live in your amazing love today.

Plant: Luke 22:14-30

Water:

» Enter it: Jesus talks in this passage about being the one who serves, even though he is the King. Why is this unusual? How do kings normally act?

» Apply it: Jesus sets us an example—even though He is our King, He loves us so much that He acts like our servant! Where is one way you can serve someone in a special way today? (Help younger children make a plan you can help them with.) As you serve, remember that Jesus is always helping you.

Weed: Where were you able to be a servant today? How did it feel to help someone? Name one idea for how you can be a servant tomorrow.

Saturday

Till: God, long, long ago you spoke in lots of different ways, at lots of different times, with one single message: a Savior is coming! And now He has come, Jesus Christ! Thank you for telling us to be on the look out for him, because He is coming again.

Plant: Luke 22:31-38

Water:

» Enter it: In today's passage, Jesus tells us that "everything written about me is now coming to a conclusion." To help kids see that all the prophets foretold Jesus, read a few prophecies with their fulfillment (with younger kids, just choose one or two): Micah 5:2, Matthew 2:1 (Born in Bethlehem) Zechariah 9:9, Matthew 21:7-8 (Jesus enters Jerusalem on a donkey) Isaiah 53:5-6, Romans 4:25 (Jesus died for our sins) Isaiah 53:8,11, Matthew 28:5-7 (Jesus rose from the dead!).

» Apply it: If Jesus fulfilled so many prophecies, then he will also make good on his promises. He is trustworthy! For example, he says, "I will never leave you or forsake you." How can you remember that Jesus is with you today?

Weed: Today we talked about how Jesus is trustworthy. Where were you able to trust him today? Name one thing you could trust him more with tomorrow.

ADVENT, WEEK 3

. . . .

Seasonal Fun:

» Advent Wreath: Each night this week light three Advent candles. Invite the oldest child to light the candles and pronounce a blessing on each of their younger siblings. Parents can set the example by blessing the eldest child first. An example of a simple blessing, "Thank you God for (child's name). You have given (child's name) the gift of (talent or gifting that child possesses.) Continue to protect and grow (child's name). Help (child's name) to use (talent or gift) to serve you and to serve others.

» Alleluia List: Remember to add to your list.

» Nativity: Each day invite the children to move the Nativity pieces a little closer to the barn.

» One night this week, gather the family around the empty barn. Give each member of the family a small handful of straw or shredded tissue paper. Invite them to help prepare for baby Jesus by filling the manger with soft material. As each member places a piece of straw into the manger share ways to prepare the heart for Jesus, too. (Some examples might be: stare at the Christmas lights and meditate on what it was like for the Shepherds to see angels, or read Luke 2:1-20, or wrap your favorite thing and give it away, just like God gave us Jesus.) Invite family members to share the ways they are preparing, or planning to prepare. Brainstorm ideas of how to prepare hearts for Jesus.

» Choose one day this week to get outside. Take a quiet walk alone or with family. Listen to God speaking as you breathe in his creation. Notice how the seasons are changing.

» Boisterous Song: *Go Tell It On the Mountain*. Sing during Advent time. If you do not know the words to this song, check out your church hymnal. If your church does not have a hymnal, "Google" the title.

» Jesse Tree: If your family is doing the Jesse Tree, here are the readings for Week Three:

  » Day 1—Scripture: 1 Kings 17:1-16, 18:17-46; Symbol: Stone Altar

  » Day 2—Scripture: 2 Kings 5:1-27; Symbol: Clean Hand

  » Day 3—Scripture: Isaiah 6:1-13; Symbol: Coal

  » Day 4—Scripture: Jeremiah 1:4-10, 2:4-13, 8:22-9:1-11; Symbol: Tears

  » Day 5—Scripture: Habakkuk 1:1-2:1, 3:16-19; Symbol: Stone Watch Tower

  » Day 6—Scripture: Nehemiah 1:1-2:8, 6:15-16, 13: 10-22; Symbol: City Wall

  » Day 7—Scripture: Hebrews 1:1-14; Symbol: Angels

Third Sunday of Advent

Till: Jesus, give us your help today. We can't do anything good without you, but with your help we can be everything you made us to be! Give us strength, and help uto notice how generous you are.

Plant: John 3:22-30

Water:

» Enter it: John the Baptist's disciples were getting jealous of Jesus, because everyone was going to Jesus instead of them! When have you felt jealous of someone else getting all the attention? Can you imagine how they felt?

» Apply it: John isn't jealous, though. He tells his disciples that the only reason he is there is to point to Jesus. So he's happy that everyone goes to Jesus! How can you make a big deal about God's love today? (Encourage kids to think of simple ways they can praise God and remind others of his love—singing songs, drawing a picture and giving it to someone, serving someone, etc.)

Weed: Where were you able to notice God's generosity today? How did that make you feel? Was there any time today that you made a big deal about you instead of God? How did that turn out? Name one idea for making a big deal about God tomorrow.

Monday
· · · · · · · ·

Till: Jesus, you trusted your Father in the most unfair situation ever. Help us to trust you when things seem unfair. Let us remember that you are still good.

Plant: Luke 22:39-53

Water:

» Imagine it: This is a sad story. First, Jesus' friends fall asleep when he asks them to keep him company! Then, one of his special followers, Judas, goes behind his back and gets him arrested. Imagine how Jesus felt.

» Apply it: Even in the midst of so much sadness, Jesus still loves people—he even heals the ear of one of the men arresting him! Jesus knew that even though this situation was very unfair, his Father still loved him. When have you felt treated unfairly? Does knowing God is still with you help when things are unfair?

Weed: What were some good things about today? What were some hard things about today? Do you think God was with you then?

Tuesday

Till: God, even though we are small, and forgetful, and make mistakes, you love us so much! You remember how we're made, that we are weak. Thank you that you always give us a new start, every day!

Plant: Luke 22:54-69

Water:

>   » Play it: To help kids understand the story, have them re-enact the scene of Peter's denial. You can read aloud the story and have them mimic their part after you. (Choose who reads Peter's part carefully—in fact, you may want to read it yourself. A sensitive child might feel very bad even pretending to deny Jesus.)

>   » Apply it: How sad! Right when Jesus is arrested, Peter (who had promised he'd never leave Jesus) denies that he even knows Jesus, to avoid being arrested too! Peter was so sad afterward. But Jesus forgave him! Can you think of a mistake that made you feel sad afterward? How does it feel to know Jesus forgives you and still loves you?

Weed: Name one thing you did well today, that made God smile. Share one mistake you made today. Let's thank God that He forgives us for that! (Lead your child in a simple prayer asking forgiveness and thanking God for his love.)

Wednesday

Till: Jesus, you came to give us a wonderful life! Life with God, life full and joyful! Thank you for changing us from the inside out!

Plant: Mark 1:1-8

Water:

> » Play it: This passage has a vivid image of making a road smooth and straight. One way to engage this is to make a rough "roadway"—have kids put toys, blocks, chairs, etc. in a hallway or path. Then have them put all the objects away while saying, "Make way! Jesus is coming!"

> » Apply it: John the Baptist came to prepare the way, a messenger with the best news ever— Jesus is coming, and he will change us from the inside out! Now Jesus has come and he is with us forever, growing us up, teaching us to love God and love others. Can you name one way you'd like to grow and be more loving? Ask Jesus for help.

Weed: When were you able to show love today? Share one situation where you'd like to love better tomorrow, with Jesus' help.

Thursday

Till: God, we want to trade in our old life for a kingdom life—a life where you are in control, always with us and always providing for us. Thank you for inviting us into your kingdom!

Plant: Matthew 3:1-12

Water:

> » Create it: John tells us that Jesus is coming to give us "Kingdom life"— life under God's care and responsibility. What is in your kingdom— what are you in charge of? Draw a picture that shows some things you

take care of, and are responsible for. (Help kids think of some things: their room, their toys, chores they do, taking care of themselves, etc.)

» Apply it: If we live in God's Kingdom, then what is He responsible for? What will God take care of?

Weed: When did you remember today that you live under God's care? Were there any hard situations that would have been different if you'd remembered that God was in control? How can you remember this tomorrow?

Friday

Till: Jesus, you're the one we've been waiting for! You know how to make everything right. Be with us today, and help us trust you always.

Plant: Matthew 11:2-15

Water:

» Create it: Jesus says that we can know he's the one we need because of what he can do: the blind see! The lame walk! Draw a picture, or create a Silly Putty sculpture, of people that Jesus has healed. What does their joy look like?

» Apply it: Jesus knows how to make everything right! What is one difficult thing in your life right now that you can trust Jesus with?

Weed: Were there any times today that you remembered to trust Jesus with a problem? How can you remember to trust Jesus tomorrow?

Saturday

Till: God, you are our Savior! You promise to save us from everything bad, in the end. Thank you! There is no one like you!

Plant: Luke 3:1-9

Water:

» Play it: Have a "parade of God's salvation"! Put on some lively kid's worship music, or make your own by singing. Dance around the house proclaiming that God saves us! How about Beethoven's *Ode to Joy*, or *Joy to the World*.

» Apply it: In today's story, John tells us that what counts is our life—is it green and blossoming? Where is your life blossoming? (Parents, this is an excellent opportunity to bless your children by pointing out what they are good at, times they are loving, qualities you admire. Take full advantage of this blessing—make sure your kids know you mean it!)

Weed: Name one way your life was blossoming and green today! Let's pray about anything we need help with. What should we ask God to help us with, since he is our savior?

ADVENT, WEEK 4

....

This week, follow the day of the week up through December 23. On December 24, use the Christmas Eve activities in the evening as well. Christmas Day and following are in the next section, Christmastide.

Seasonal fun:

» Advent Wreath: Each night until Christmas Eve light four Advent candles. Invite everyone to sit at the table in total darkness. While lighting the first candle, say "Jesus brings his light to our dark world." Say while lighting the remaining candles, "And we will pass his light on and on and on." Invite different family members to light the candles in this manner each night.

» Alleluia List: Remember to add to your list.

» Nativity: Move the animals into the barn.

» Give: Invite the whole family to make homemade gifts (a plate of cookies, cranberry bread, etc). It wasn't that long ago in our culture that homemade gifts were given to the mailperson, to firefighters, to neighbors. Ask the children to help you listen to the Holy Spirit, then ask, "Who would you like for us to bless with homemade gifts?" Brainstorm a list of a three or four people that you would not normally give gifts to. It is important that all members of the family help. It may look the best if Mom does it all, but "looking" the best is not the most important thing here. A family opportunity to bless others is the main idea.

» Consider fasting TV this week. The children will be out of school this week; give them the gift of listening, the gift of your full attention.

» Boisterous Song: *Angels We Have Heard on High*. Sing during Advent time. If you do not know the words to this song, check out your church hymnal. If your church does not have a hymnal, "Google" the title.

» Jesse Tree: If your family is doing the Jesse Tree, here are the readings for Week Four:

    » Day 1—Scripture: Luke 1:57-80; Symbol: Dove

    » Day 2—Scripture: Luke 1:26-38; Symbol: White Lily

    » Day 3—Scripture: Luke 1:39-56; Symbol: Mother and Child

    » Day 4—Scripture: Luke 1:57-80; Symbol: Pencil and Tablet

    » Day 5—Scripture: Matthew 1:18-25; Symbol: Hammer

    » Day 6—Scripture: Matthew 2:1-12; Symbol: Candle

Fourth Sunday of Advent

Till: Good morning God! Thank you that we're waking up to your love. You love us so much you gave your Son, so we could have whole, lasting life with you! You came to help us, Jesus! Please be with us and help us today, Holy Spirit.

Plant: John 3:16-21

Water:

» Create it: God loves the world! And he sent his Son, Jesus, into the world to save it. Draw a picture that shows the world and expresses God's love for us.

» Apply it: Jesus came to help us and give us life. In today's passage, though, he points out that to receive his help we have to admit that we need it, and come to him. Can you think of a time you didn't want to ask for help, even though you needed it? What do you need God's help with today?

Weed: Where did you need God's help today? Were you able to ask? Let's ask God for help with tomorrow. What do you need help with then?

Monday
· · · · · · · ·

Till: Jesus, you made us, you help us, you love us. You introduce us to your Father! Help us to know you more, and to know your Father more, through the help of your Spirit.

Plant: John 5:30-47

Water:

» Apply it: Jesus tells us that the Bible is all about him, and that He is where we find full life! What are some things you know about Jesus? Talk about him for a little while.

Weed: Share one reason you are thankful for Jesus today. What is one way you can spend time with Jesus tomorrow?

Tuesday
· · · · · · · ·

Till: God, when things look hopeless to us, you're just getting started. You love surprising us with your goodness! Help us to be on the lookout for surprising goodness today.

Plant: Luke 1:5-25

Water:

» Play it: Help your children re-enact the scene! You can read the story and have them mimic the action as you go along. You'll need a Zachariah, an Elizabeth and an Angel.

» Apply it: When the angel told Zachariah his wife Elizabeth would have a baby, he just couldn't believe it! How could this be—they were too old! But God loves to do surprising things, where we think it's hopeless. What is a situation that seems like it's too hard for you to handle alone? Ask God to do something surprising there.

Weed: Where were you surprised by God's love or goodness today? How could you be on the lookout for God's surprises more tomorrow?

Wednesday

Till: Father God, we are your little servants. Let your good plans for us go just as you want them to. We'll follow you!

Plant: Luke 1:26-38

Water:

» Play it: Help your children re-enact the scene! You can read the story and have them mimic the action as you go along. You'll need a Mary and an angel Gabriel.

» Apply it: When an angel showed up and told Mary she was going to have a baby—the Son of God, Jesus!—she was surprised but obedient. She said, "I'm ready to serve." Where can you be obedient today?

Weed: When were you able to be obedient today? When was it hard to obey? What is one way you'd like to be more obedient tomorrow?

Thursday

Till: We love you God! You make us dance with joy because you do amazing things. Hooray for God!

Plant: Luke 1:39-56

Water:

> » Play it: Mary bursts into song in praise of God, because he provided a Savior, Jesus! Sing and dance with thankfulness to God today, either to a kids' worship CD or while making your own song.

> » Imagine it: Picture, in your mind, Mary and Elizabeth—the mothers of Jesus and John the Baptist—starting to understand that God was going to change the world forever through their children. How do you think they felt? How did they feel toward God?

Weed: Share one time you felt thankful to God today, or one thing you are thankful for. When did you forget to be thankful? How can you remember to rejoice in God tomorrow?

Friday

Till: God, your ways are good. It's always best to follow you and trust, because you know what's good for us. Help us to trust you today.

Plant: Luke 1:57-66

Water:

> » Enter it: Remember back a few days ago, when we read about the angel telling Zachariah his wife would have a baby? Because he didn't believe it, God took away his voice until the baby was born. What do you think that was like? What do you think Zachariah learned while he silently waited for his miracle child to be born?

» Apply it: One of the things Zachariah learned was that it is always best to trust God—that's why he named the baby John just as he was instructed. What is something you can trust God with today?

Weed: Where did you trust God today? What did you do to obey him? When did you feel afraid? How could you remember God's trustworthiness tomorrow?

Christmas Eve
. . . .

Seasonal Fun:

» Advent Wreath: Light all four candles. Some families celebrate Christmas on this eve, others wait until Christmas morning. If your family celebrates this Eve, light the Jesus candle as well.

» Nativity: Move Mary and Joseph into the barn, but don't put baby Jesus in the manger yet (unless you celebrate Christmas on this Eve— then go ahead and put him in.)

» Alleluia List: Display your Alleluia lists in a place that will remind everyone to be an Alleluia from head to toe.

» Boisterous Song: *O Little Town of Bethlehem*. Sing during Advent time. If you do not know the words to this song, check out your church hymnal. If your church does not have a hymnal, "Google" the title.

CHRISTMASTIDE

....

Introduction to Christmastide

The Light of God has come into the world and it's time to celebrate! It is in Jesus' life that we find life. It is in his coming that we find our relationship with God restored. In him we live and move and have our being. So if you've got dancin' shoes, this is the season to put them on! The long awaited Son of God is here and it's time to celebrate!

In modern times Christmas has been reduced to one day, but that has not always been so. Twelve full days (remember the song *The Twelve Days of Christmas*?) was the traditional length of celebration, from Christmas Day until Epiphany on January 6. Now though, most folks have to return to work during those twelve days. Most of us begin to celebrate Christmas shortly after Thanksgiving; we have been "celebrating" for a month or more already. So when the wonderful day of Christ's birth is here, we are ready to get it over with and move on. Who can blame us?

But our church fathers knew that celebration is more deeply enjoyed when waiting has occurred. If we have observed the weeks of Advent longing, by Christmas we are more than ready to party. How about a twelve-day celebration? God is with us—Immanuel—and twelve days doesn't seem nearly enough.

Warning! We are giving your family many, many, suggestions for celebration; please don't attempt to do them all. Choose a few, maybe only one. We crazy human beings have a tendency toward overkill. We all have the inclination to force those around us into the "happiest Christmas they've ever had." Do your family a favor and give that up. Pray over all the options you will read about and invite the Holy Spirit to guide you. He will. He loves your family, too.

Soil Care and Tools

I (Lacy) have planted three—count 'em, three—raspberry bushes in the same spot. The spot gets great sun; the bushes around it grow just fine. But in this one spot, they die. I think it's the soil. Something toxic is in this dirt, or maybe it's just bad soil. Our souls are often this way as well. We keep trying to plant kindness, or gentleness, but death is all we reap. This Baby we celebrate came to bring us abundant life. Only he can make us whole; only he can fill our soul with what is so desperately missing. But we need tools to deliver these nutrients. Richard Foster discusses these tools in his book, *Celebration of Discipline.*[1] Lucky enough for us, he provides twelve tools and we have twelve days of Christmas. He calls these tools "Spiritual Disciplines." During Christmastide we will explore them, seeing what they look like used by a family.

As we learn and practice the Spiritual Disciplines we will use kid-friendly definitions. Valerie Hess also has a great book about living the disciplines with your children called *Habits of a Child's Heart.*[2] But for an in-depth study and a wonderful book, check out *Celebration of Discipline.*

In *Celebration of Discipline,* the disciplines are grouped by inner, outer, and corporate disciplines. This follows the natural progress of life in human beings: First our inner life (heart) is changed, then our outer life (body) follows. It's only then that we can live it out corporately with those who surround us. In what follows we will follow that progression as well. Nature also teaches us this. What we do to the soil is lived out in the stem, leaves, flowers, fruit or lack thereof. So my raspberry plants are teaching me.

Each day of Christmastide will feature one of the disciplines, with ideas of how to engage it with your little ones. But be creative. These tools are meant to work for you, not overwhelm you!

---

1 Richard J. Foster, *Celebration of Discipline.* HarperCollins. 2002.
2 Valerie Hess, *Habits of a Child's Heart.* NavPress. 2004.

About the Christmastide Readings

For these twelve days, the daily Scripture readings break down into two different themes. For the first set of six days, we read the Christmas story and then watch the characters' various reactions to it: Stephen and the children of Bethlehem give their lives; Herod and the Pharisees are angry; some come to the light but others prefer the darkness. With these readings, we find that like Mary we treasure up the Christmas story in our hearts and ponder: what will our response be?

For the second set of six days, the readings center around the "I Am" statements in the book of John. Jesus declares himself to be the Bread of Life, the Vine, the Gate, the Good Shepherd, the Road, Truth, and Life, the Resurrection, and the Light of the World. With each of these declarations, Jesus also proclaims that he is "I AM"—God incarnate! With these readings, we marvel at who this One Who Came Among Us shows himself to be. To help kids understand these, create a wall mural: Put up a large sign declaring "I AM!" Each day kids can draw a picture of how Jesus describes himself, and add it to the growing mural on the wall.

Celebration

In many families people have to work on Christmas or soon after, so our suggestion is to have one big day of celebration and eleven other small celebrations. My husband sometimes must work on Christmas Day, though he might have the 24th or the 26th off, so we schedule the big celebration for one of the days he has off.

Like all of the seasons of the church, Christmastide has a color: white, for the purity of Christ. During these twelve days we break out white napkins, tablecloth, and white candles—even the white china, because only the best will do for the King of Kings. Even on the small celebration days we use the good dishes. It reminds us that, despite work or other obligations, all twelve days of Christmastide are celebrations.

Boisterous Singing

No celebration is complete without boisterous singing. Let loose, even if your family has absolutely no singing abilities or even the desire to sing. Give it a try and see if by doing it, you don't learn to love it.

No Christmastide celebration is complete without the song *The Twelve Days of Christmas*. Many of our traditions have their roots in pagan customs, and *The Twelve Days of Christmas* is no different. But like Easter eggs and the Christmas tree, *The Twelve Days of Christmas* has been redeemed.

Some say that the words of the song were secret code for people to remember their faith during times of persecution. Whether or not this explanation is true, the song is a great tool for learning and remembering what is important about our faith. We are including the words to the song, along with the secret code for remembering our faith.

The Twelve Days of Christmas

A Partridge in a Pear Tree
The partridge in a pear tree is Jesus the Christ, the Son of God, whose birthday we celebrate on December 25, the first day of Christmas. In the song, Christ is symbolically presented as a mother partridge that feigns injury to divert predators from her helpless nestlings, recalling Christ's sadness over the fate of Jerusalem: "Jerusalem! Jerusalem! How often would I have sheltered you under my wings, as a hen does her chicks, but you would not have it so . . . ." (Luke 13:34)

Two Turtle Doves
The two turtle doves are the Old and New Testaments, which together bear witness to God's self-revelation in history and the creation of a people to tell the Story of God to the world.

Three French Hens
The three French hens refer to the three theological virtues of 1 Corinthians 13:13: faith, hope, and love.

Four Calling Birds

The four calling birds are the four gospels—Matthew, Mark, Luke, and John—which proclaim the Good News of God's reconciliation of the world to himself in Jesus Christ.

Five Gold Rings

The five gold rings are the first five books of the Old Testament, known as the Torah or the Pentateuch. They are Genesis, Exodus, Leviticus, Numbers, and Deuteronomy, which together give the history of humanity's sinful failure and God's response of grace in the creation of a people to be a light to the world.

Six Geese A-Laying

The six geese represent the whole six days of creation that confesses God as Creator and Sustainer of the world (Genesis 1).

Seven Swans A-Swimming

The seven swimming swans are the seven gifts of the Holy Spirit identified by Paul: prophecy, ministry, teaching, exhortation, generosity, leadership, and compassion (Romans 12:6-8 and 1 Corinthians 12:8-11).

Eight Maids A-Milking

The eight maids represent the eight Beatitudes: Blessed are 1) the poor in spirit, 2) those who mourn, 3) the meek, 4) those who hunger and thirst for righteousness, 5) the merciful, 6) the pure in heart, 7) the peacemakers, 8) those who are persecuted for righteousness' sake (Matthew 5:3-10).

Nine Ladies Dancing

The nine dancing ladies are the nine fruits of the Holy Spirit: love, joy, peace, patience, kindness, generosity, faithfulness, gentleness, and self-control (Galatians 5:22).

Ten Lords A-Leaping

The ten lords are the ten commandments: 1) You shall have no other gods before me; 2) Do not make an idol; 3) Do not take God's name in vain; 4) Remember the Sabbath Day; 5) Honor your father and mother;

6) Do not murder; 7) Do not commit adultery; 8) Do not steal; 9) Do not bear false witness; 10) Do not covet (Exodus 20:1-17).

Eleven Pipers Piping

The eleven pipers are the eleven faithful Apostles: Simon Peter, Andrew, James, John, Philip, Bartholomew, Matthew, Thomas, James bar Alphaeus, Simon the Zealot, Judas bar James (Luke 6:14-16). The list does not include the twelfth original Disciple, Judas Iscariot, who betrayed Jesus to the religious leaders and the Romans.

Twelve Drummers Drumming

Finally, the twelve drummers are the twelve points of doctrine in the Apostles' Creed:

1) I believe in God, the Father almighty, creator of heaven and earth.

2) I believe in Jesus Christ, his only Son, our Lord.

3) He was conceived by the power of the Holy Spirit and born of the virgin Mary.

4) He suffered under Pontius Pilate, was crucified, died, and was buried. He descended into hell [the grave].

5) On the third day he rose again. He ascended into heaven, and is seated at the right hand of the Father.

6) He will come again to judge the living and the dead.

7) I believe in the Holy Spirit, 8) the holy catholic Church, 9) the communion of saints, 10) the forgiveness of sins, 11) the resurrection of the body, 12) and the life everlasting.

Christmastide Seasonal Fun

» Wait to decorate your family tree until Christmas morning. Or, that morning add a special finishing touch, such as a garland, or special ornaments like angels and stars.

» Spread the opening of presents out over twelve days. One advantage of this practice is frugality. Most stores deeply discount their inventory after the 25th.

» Share in the joy of creation with our Creator, and make homemade gifts.

» Gather the children around and create a Joy Jar. Choose a jar; a particularly beautiful jar would make a great Christmas gift. Give each member of the family small strips of paper. Instruct everyone to write down one thing they would love to do during Christmastide, such as go to a movie, or take a quiet walk, or play a game, or go bowling, or read a book together. It must be something the whole family can do together. Put all the slips in the jar and mix them up. Each day during Christmastide, choose a slip and do the activity.

» Assign parts and act out the Christmas story. This can be wonderfully funny (assign wacky parts, like barn animals), or very serious and solemn: your choice.

» Invite friends over to light candles and sing songs.

» Light all four candles and the Christ candle on the Advent wreath, if you usually only light the middle Christ candle on Christmas.

» Light twelve candles, one for each of the twelve days of Christmastide.

» Join in the tradition of families gathering greens and dried fruit and then making wreaths out of them. Put them up on Christmas Eve and left them up through Christmastide.

» Eat a Yule Log! Originally the Yule Log was just that—a log. A very large log. One end was pushed into the fireplace and burned, while the rest of it just lay out in the middle of the room. As more heat was needed during the twelve day celebration it was pushed further into the fire. For various reasons (think fire hazard!), the tradition morphed into a pastry log as a symbol of Christmastide. Yule Logs can be bought or their creation assigned to the family teenagers.

» Invite the children to create a poster of the song *The Twelve Days of Christmas* using poster board and markers. Be sure to include the words and the secret code. Use it to sing by each evening of Christmastide.

12 DAYS OF CHRISTMAS

Christmas Day (December 25)

Christmas Day Fun

» Advent Wreath: If you have a Christ candle in the middle of your Advent wreath, this is the day to light it.

» Nativity: First thing this morning, put baby Jesus in the manger. Some families may be so excited about Christmas morning that it becomes the perfect opportunity for a family dance! Others may be overwhelmed by the beauty of the birth of Christ, warranting silence.

» Boisterous Singing: *Joy to the World*. If you do not know the words to this song, check out your church hymnal. If your church does not have a hymnal, "google" the title.

Tool: The inner discipline of **prayer**. It's an old tool that may need to be re-tooled. Prayer is talking to God. Today invite your children to do all the praying. Offer prayers of thanksgiving at different intervals throughout the day. Try praying without much formality. No need to bow the head or close the eyes, just say aloud a conversational prayer of thanks whenever the mood strikes.

Till: Happy birthday, Jesus! Immanuel—God, you are with us! Thank you for being near to us always. Help us remember that you are close by, no matter where we go.

Plant: Matthew 1:18-25

Water:

» Play it: Have the children act out the manger scene! Let one of the kids be the director.

» Apply it: In the Bible, Jesus is called Immanuel, which means "God is with us." And He is! What is one way you can remember that God is with you throughout today? (Set a hourly timer, put a picture/symbol someplace visible, etc. Make this a game!)

Weed: How did your game of remembering God-with-you go today? Was it easy, or hard? What is another way you can remember that God is with you tomorrow? How can you carry your conversation with God into tomorrow?

December 26 (Feast of Stephen)

The day after Christmas has long been dedicated to remembering Stephen, the first Christian martyr. By putting Christmas and the Feast of Stephen together, the Church remembers what our response to God's gift should be: like Stephen, we are to offer him everything we are! Gather the family around and read Acts 6:8-7:60. This is a very long passage and small children may lose interest, but for older children Stephen is a wonderful example of a man who knew his faith and knew how to live and die like Jesus.

Tool: The inner discipline of **meditation**. Meditation has gotten a bad rap among Christians in recent years. This is unfortunate, because meditation is simply to focus our minds on God and his words to us. Children have an awesome ability to meditate. If you have ever walked to the driveway with a toddler only to have them wander away and stare at a line of ants, you have seen meditation. They are focused entirely (despite your cries, and threats) on the little red insects.

Till: Jesus, today we remember your bold witness, Stephen. Help us to stand for you with boldness and courage.

Plant: Acts 6:8–7:60

Water:

» Imagine it: Share what you would have done if you were in Stephen's place. Could you forgive like him? How do you think he became so much like Jesus?

» Apply it: Can you explain your faith as well as Stephen? If not, what could you do to change that?

Weed: What was one way you were able to trust God today, even though it was hard? How could you remember to trust God in hard choices tomorrow? Tools can be misused: Are there things that you meditated on that aren't good for you?

December 27

Tool: The inner discipline of **study**. Among school age children study can be a dirty word. However studying about God doesn't always require a book. Although the best book to study is the Bible, there are other ways to learn about God, Jesus and the Holy Spirit. One way is to study God's creation. In Acts the disciples described the coming of the Holy Spirit as wind. Spend some time standing in the wind; focus all your senses on this experience. Next time you read the Scriptures about the Holy Spirit, you will have a memory stored that will bring the Scriptures to life.

Till: Jesus, you are the greatest gift we could ever get, because you bring us God's love—over the top, constant love! Thank you for coming to us!

Plant: John 3:31-36

Water:

» Apply it: Today we celebrate God's gift to us, Jesus! What are some gifts God has given you that you are thankful for?

» Enter it: In many cultures, the time after Christmas is used to give something away. After a big day of receiving presents, kids can benefit a lot from giving. Help kids each select something (in reasonably good condition) you can donate, maybe a neglected toy or game that would make another child very happy. Or, collect some canned goods to donate to a food pantry.

» Study it: Light a candle or a fireplace and spend some time studying the firelight. Notice the colors, the sounds, the smells. Without burning yourselves, feel the heat. What is it about light and fire that reminds us of Jesus?

Weed: What are you most thankful for today? What is one way you can practice giving (time, help, gifts) to show love tomorrow?

December 28 (Feast of the Innocents)

Gather the family together to read Matthew 2:13-23. This is an extremely sad story. It is good for us to remember during our celebrations that there are those throughout the world who cannot celebrate as we do. It is a time to remember the many refugees who have no home and may have lost their family. It is a time to remember the many children who are taken advantage of, abused, and orphaned in our world.

This day is also a day of action. Commit as a family to stay informed about the state of refugees around the world. World Vision and International Justice Mission are good organizations with which to stay informed and to give money, plus they keep people informed about how to pray. If your children are older, consider spending a few Saturdays, or even vacation time, helping out in a soup kitchen. Consider sponsoring a child through Compassion International. In showing compassion to others we show compassion to Christ.

The Scripture lesson reminds us that as we open our hearts, minds, and pocketbooks to those who cannot celebrate on this day, we open to Christ who also was a refugee and a hunted child. It is in giving that we receive; it is in dying that we live.

Tool: The inner discipline of **fasting**. There is no better way to share in sorrow than to fast. Fasting is a natural response to deep sorrow. Today we will read of Herod's horrible slaughter of the innocent children while in search of Jesus. In the midst of our Christmastide celebration, we do not forget those who suffer, or those for whom celebration is not possible. Fasting is giving up something on purpose so we can hear God. Discuss one thing your family needs to give up for good, or for a period of time, to hear God better. Fasting totally from food is not advisable for children; instead consider eating only oatmeal at all meals today to develop empathy for those that eat this every day. Consider fasting your time by volunteering at a soup kitchen as a family.

Till: Father, help us to celebrate with those who are happy, and weep with those who are sad, so that we share your tender heart with everyone. You are compassionate.

Plant: Matthew 2:13-23

Water:

» Enter it: Tell about a time when you were most afraid. How do you think Mary and Joseph must have felt while running for their lives? Tell about a time when someone you loved died, pet or human. Imagine how the mothers and fathers of Bethlehem must have felt.

» Apply it: Invite older children to search the newspaper for instances that remind them of today's reading. Brainstorm ways to alleviate suffering in your town and around the world. The solutions may be outside the home, like volunteering to teach English to immigrants, or a little closer, like checking the newspaper weekly and holding a family prayer time for those who are suffering. This may seem like a hard topic for children, but it is children who possess the hope and faith to follow Jesus in compassion.

Weed: Where did you see or hear about suffering today? How did it make you feel? What can you do? Share about a time you experienced suffering? How did you know that God was with you?

December 29
. . . .

Tool: The outer discipline of **simplicity**. We are now moving from the inner disciplines to the outer disciplines. Through prayer, meditation, study and fasting God has improved our soul soil. Now we will see some sprouts of new life beginning to break the surface. One of those sprouts is simplicity. Simplicity is letting go of things that keep us from God. Simplicity is letting the main thing be the main thing. In simplicity we teach our children to speak directly and honestly without shading the truth to make themselves look better. In simplicity we limit distractions, and tear down our idols willingly and with joy.

Till: God, thank you for being our father who is always with us. Thank you that Jesus came so that we could know you ourselves!

Plant: John 16:23b-30

Water:

» Apply it: In today's reading, Jesus explains to his disciples that He came from God the Father so we could know God directly—and that will be a wonderful life! Can you think of some things that you know about God because Jesus showed them to us?

» Draw it: Draw a picture of what you imagine it will be like to live with God. In your picture, include some of your favorite people from the Bible—like Abraham, or Noah, or David, or Mary—because they will be there too.

» Simplify it: What is a distraction to obeying God in your life? Do you have any possessions that own you? Consider giving them away.

Weed: Share about a time you thought about God today. Where did you feel his love? What is one activity tomorrow that you'd like to do with God? Tell about a time today when you were distracted from hearing God. Is there anything you need to do about this?

December 30
· · · · · · · · · · · · · · · ·

Tool: The outer discipline of **solitude**. Last night as I was tucking my daughter in for the night she said, "I need some Mommy time." She's not alone: human beings crave intimate relationships. Solitude opens the space for intimate relationship with God through quiet, private time with him. Using the inner disciplines we talked with God, gave up things that kept us from him, thought about him, and even studied him to the point that it has grown into a love relationship where we want to spend quiet alone time with him.

Till: God, you fill us and fill us with your love and Spirit so we can overflow and overflow to others. Help us to love others well today!

Plant: John 7:37–43

Water:

» Create it: A good visual to help you understand the overflow of God's love is to get a glass or a jar, and in the sink let it fill up with water then overflow. Keep running water into it. Then, place another container under it—a bowl, for instance—that can catch the overflow. Discuss with kids how God's love fills us so there's enough to give to others!

» Apply it: Can you name someone that you would like God's love to spill over onto from your heart? Maybe someone that is challenging to love? How can you remember that God is with you as you love them?

» Make it: Sometimes quiet, alone time is hard to find, especially in a family. Designate one corner or chair as "with God" space. Whenever someone is in that space, no one is to bother them. Try to get to that space at least once a day.

Weed: Where did you overflow love to others today? Was it hard to be nice to anyone today? Let's pray and ask Jesus to teach us to love this person. When did you find time to be alone with God today?

December 31 (New Year's Eve)

While New Year's Eve is not an explicitly Christian tradition, it is an American one. Plan a family party: snacks, hats, decorations. Encourage children to invite friends, play games. Smooch the ones you love as the New Year bells chime.

Tool: The outer discipline of **service**. Service is just like it sounds: doing something for others. Families function well when the spirit of serving each other pervades. Richard Foster discusses service within families in his book, *The Challenge of the Disciplined Life*.[3] Here he outlines how parents serve their children: "by providing purposeful leadership, through compassionate discipline, by giving them a growing self-governance, by being available and vulnerable, by respecting them, and by introducing them to the spiritual life." Also how children serve their parents: "by being obedient, through respect, by meekly refusing to do what is clearly destructive, and by caring for their needs when the dependency roles are reversed." While service outside of the home is clearly part of God's redemptive plan, true service begins by serving those closest to us.

Till: Jesus, Light of the World, come today and shine your light in our lives! Light up our path so we can follow you.

Plant: John 8:12-19   *I Am the Light of the World*

Water:

» Create it: This is the first of six days where we will be reading Jesus' "I Am" statements from the Gospel of John. Invite children to draw a picture, or make a Silly Putty sculpture that expresses the truth that

---

3 Richard J. Foster, *The Challenge of the Disciplined Life*. HarperCollins. 1989.

Jesus is our Light. Each day, put the picture or sculpture on display and add to it.

» Apply it: What are some situations you find confusing? How can you ask Jesus to shine his light there today?

» Serve it: As a family, take another look at the tool of service. In what way are you doing well serving each other? In what ways do you need to improve?

Weed: What ways did knowing Jesus help you to live well today? How did He light up your path? Were there any times you avoided seeing his light today so you could do what you wanted instead of what God wanted? Let's ask God's forgiveness, and thank him for his patience.

January 1 (New Year's Day)

Celebrating the New Year is not a Christian tradition. Still, New Year's Day can be an excellent day for taking stock of family priorities, goals and visions. David Robinson's book, *The Busy Family's Guide to Spirituality*[4] helps families set rhythms and visions that lead to Christ. *Parenting by Developmental Design*[5] by Vivian L. Houk is also a good book for establishing the spiritual formation of children in the home. Today is the day to see some visions, set some goals and write them down.

Tool: The outer discipline of **submission**. Submission, giving up our own way, can be a tough tool to use, which is why we must have the inner tools of prayer, meditation, fasting and study first. Giving up getting our way deals a death blow to our preoccupation with self. Submission can teach lifelong lessons to squabbling siblings. Learning through submission to be peacemakers moves our children and indeed ourselves into a greater place of becoming true children of God. We teach our children to submit to us, but we also need to be aware and practice submission to our children. Submission is not a position of

---

4 David Robinson, *The Busy Family's Guide to Spirituality*. Crossroads. 2009.
5 Vivian L. Houk, *Parenting by Developmental Design*. Resource Publications. 2010.

weakness, like the world would have us believe, but a place where the strength and purposes of God find their home.

Till: Jesus, you are the Resurrection—new life where we don't see any hope. Help us to live in hope of your amazing power to give life! You submitted to God and came to Earth to be a human. Thank you for showing us how to submit. Teach us to submit to you and to each other.

Plant: John 11:17-27, 38-44   *I Am the Resurrection and the Life*

Water:

- » Create it: Invite children to draw a picture, or make a Silly Putty sculpture that expresses the truth that Jesus is our New Life. One helpful image that kids can understand is the changing of seasons. Right now, in winter, most things have lost leaves and look dead. But they will be green in the springtime! Invite kids to relate this idea of new life to the start of a new year.

- » Apply it: Are there any situations where you feel like giving up, like there's no hope? This new year, how can you remember Jesus' amazing power to bring new life to those situations? Let's ask for his help.

- » Submit it: Mom and Dad can confess to your children the ways that you have not been submissive to them. (Maybe being too controlling? Maybe insisting on doing an activity that you enjoy instead of one that they enjoy?) Pray together and ask God to show you some areas where submission needs to grow.

- » Act it: Invite the children to help you write a short skit about something they normally fight over. This time though, have one child let the other have their way. Act out the natural conclusion to the fight when submission is involved. Act out the skit a second time, having the opposite child submit. Discuss other areas where submission is needed.

Weed: Did knowing Jesus give you hope in any situations today? How does it help to know that He is the Resurrection and the Life? Where were you feeling like giving up today? Tell about a time when you had the chance to submit.

January 2

Tool: The corporate discipline of **confession**. Confession is admitting to God and to others when we have done something wrong. God used the tools of prayer, meditation, fasting and study to improve our soul soil, which led to small sprouts of service, simplicity, solitude, and submission. And now we have the fruit of confession, the fruit that comes from using the other tools. Confession is simply admitting the truth. More than once I've been lost at an amusement park and refused to admit it. Until I admit I have no idea where I am, I can never be found; I just keep wandering around looking at the same ice cream stand! Confession is saying, "Wow, I'm lost. I made some wrong turns and I need help to get out of here." Sometimes we say this to God, and sometimes we say this to others. When we offer forgiveness to people, we give them the map to be found. When God offers us forgiveness, he finds us.

Till: Jesus, you are the Bread of Life—we hunger for meaning, love, and your presence, and you fill us up like a great feast! Feed us today, both our bodies and our hearts.

Plant: John 6:35–41, 48–51   *I Am the Bread of Life*

Water:

» Create it: Invite children to draw a picture, or make a Silly Putty sculpture that expresses the truth that Jesus is the Bread of Life.

» Apply it: Jesus promises that he will, himself, take care of all our needs. What we need most is him! Can you come up with an idea of how to remember He is caring for your needs today?

Weed: How were you able to remember Jesus taking care of you today? Spend a few quiet minutes telling God where you were wrong today. Do you need to say you were wrong to your family members?

January 3

Tool: The corporate discipline of **worship**. Worship is our response to God who loves us. Worship is Moses ripping off his shoes in response to a God who spoke directly to him. Worship is a room full of preschoolers dancing a jig while singing *Jesus Loves the Little Children*. Worship is teenagers falling strangely silent as they approach a mountain precipice that dwarfs their egos. Worship is the family that gives up their Saturday morning pancakes to work in a soup kitchen, knowing God has supplied all their needs. Worship is sweet, nourishing fruit that we can't live without.

Till: Jesus, you are the doorway into God's love, and you're also the shepherd that cares for us! Thank you for always protecting and caring for us, and being with us today.

Plant: John 10:7–17 *I am the Gate of the Sheep; I Am the Good Shepherd*

Water:

> » Create it: Invite children to draw a picture, or make a Silly Putty sculpture that expresses the truth that Jesus is the Gate and the Shepherd of the Sheep.

> » Imagine it: The 23rd Psalm is one of the most treasured passages of Scripture because it describes God as our Good Shepherd. Read this passage slowly to your children and invite them to imagine each scene, one by one. Ask which part they like the most.

> » Worship him: We are in the season of Christmastide: it is the season for worship! Gather together various art materials and invite family members to respond to, or worship Jesus, Immanuel, God with us. Display their art throughout Christmastide and on into Epiphany.

Weed: Before bedtime, read over the 23rd Psalm again, slowly, imagining each scene. Remind your children that God is always with them, leading them like a Good Shepherd. In what ways did you worship today?

January 4

Tool: The corporate tool of **guidance**. Guidance is listening to the counsel of God and others who love us. Each night before I go to bed, I go outside and make a last check of all the animals. Here in the country there are no outside lights. Robert Frost is right that "the woods are lovely dark and deep," but I would like to add that without a light, they are dangerous. Sometimes my fears are about real things, like that coyote that I hear howl as I make my rounds, and sometimes they are imagined—the branches that look like monsters ready to pounce. However, if I grab a flashlight as I head out the door all things change. I know where I am at all times, wild animals generally run from light, and those imaginary monsters simply don't exist. Guidance is a light. Often through the scriptures God lights our paths, while through the advice of others he keeps us safe. Guidance is a light we receive and a light we give away.

Till: Jesus, you are the Road that leads us to Truth and Life! Help us to follow closely and not stray from you today.

Plant: John 14:6-14   *I am the Road, the Truth, the Life*

Water:

> » Create it: Invite children to draw a picture, or make a Silly Putty sculpture that expresses the truth that Jesus is the Road, the Truth, and the Life.

> » Apply it: Jesus shows us the way to God—in fact, he even says that when we look at him, we know what God is like. What is one way Jesus teaches us to live? How can you follow him in that today?

> » Try it: Blindfold one member of your family, and bake cookies or wash the supper dishes together. (Don't use your good dishes.) Take turns changing who is blindfolded. Discuss the parallel of Jesus being the light, and us needing light to see.

> » Take a hike: Set aside sometime this week to find some an outdoor space and take a hike. If you live in a snowy area, rent snowshoes. Talk about following the map, staying on the trail, Jesus being our guide, and taking guidance from others.

Weed: How did you do in following Jesus in the area you named earlier today? Can you think of a way you would like to follow Jesus even more closely tomorrow?

January 5 (Eve of Epiphany)

It is the last day of Christmastide. Time to pack up all the lovelies, greenery, lights, candles, and the good dishes. But it's not a solemn occasion. The last of the Christmastide treats must be eaten and this is the day. Singing boisterous songs and finishing up tasty snacks can move the process along quite nicely. When the last box is packed and the last fingers are licked gather everyone together to breathe a prayer of thanksgiving for the many blessings of Christmastide.

Tool: The corporate tool of **celebration**. Celebration is knowing that every good gift is from God and a reason to party! We have worked with God to use the tools of prayer, fasting, meditation, and study to deeply feed our soul soil, and that led to little sprouts of simplicity, service, solitude and submission. When those matured we harvested the fruit of confession, worship and guidance. Everybody knows that a party follows harvest time! It's time to celebrate all the hard work, dedication, and ultimately God's provision and goodness. Our good God has taken our toxic soil and made it well. He has taken death and made life. It's a "pinch-me-I'm-dreaming" reality.

Till: Jesus, you are the Vine, and we are branches that grow from you and bear fruit! Help us to stay connected to you and produce lots of fruit!

Plant: John 15:1-16   *I Am the Vine*

Water:

» Create it: Invite children to draw a picture or make a Silly Putty sculpture that expresses the truth that Jesus is the Vine, and we are the branches.

» Apply it: Jesus tells us to "abide" in him. That means to stay very close to him always. Brainstorm some ways you can remember Jesus throughout today.

» Plan it: Tomorrow is Epiphany. Plan an Epiphany party, complete with music, games, and snacks. Let the children decorate. Invite the neighbors.

» Plant it: We need to be reminded that Jesus is all about life. In the winter months remembering this can be difficult. Force some bulbs; Amaryllis or Paperwhites are particularly easy and lovely this time of year. We also like to plant a pot of lettuce or spinach indoors. The kids care for it and watch it grow, and then we harvest it and it gives us life. It's a very good, hands-on lesson of how God cares for us.

Weed: When did you stay close to Jesus today? When did you forget? Can you think of a way we can remind each other to abide in Jesus tomorrow? Choose one of the twelve tools, and ask God to help you use it tomorrow. Make a verbal list of all that you have been thankful for during Christmastide. Turn your list into a prayer.

EPIPHANY

....

Epiphany is the season when we embrace Jesus as the gift, not just to us, but to the whole world. It's like we're saying, "'He's got the whole world in his hands...' Sing along with us!" When the Magi arrived from distant lands, it was a major sign that this was not just a small town boy born into a one-nation religion. Jesus was the One to show that "God so loved the world...."

I (Lacy) forget this far too often, living in my one horse town, attending my very American church. I forget that I'm only one child in a family that's several millennia old and spans seven continents. (As far as I can tell, the penguins living in Antarctica are God-fearing and I'm including them.) In the last twenty years or so it has been my great delight to discover my amazing brothers and sisters, past and present, and realize that I'm part of a huge, everlasting plan that can't be contained by space or time.

During Epiphany we focus on the life of Jesus and how he lived in the Kingdom of God here on earth. The word "epiphany" comes from a Greek word that means "to show." During Epiphany we think about how Jesus showed himself to be God's Son. We think about how to show ourselves to be God's children. We think about how to show the nations that God loves them.

This Epiphany we're going to take a little "walk" around the globe, praying for and learning about our not-so-distant family members. Each Sunday we will remember a different continent. If you don't already have one, you might invest in a globe or a large map of the world to help you envision the place and the people.

About Epiphany

The day of Epiphany, January 6, is the day we celebrate the Magi worshipping Jesus. With them, we discover that Jesus comes to make God known to all nations. This day is marked with merriment and ceremonies. We start with the official celebration of Epiphany on January 6, move through the daily rhythms of Ordinary Time (those weeks that fall between the special seasons of Advent/Christmas and Lent/Easter), then end just before Ash Wednesday.

The color of Epiphany is green. Winter's full force is upon us now, and the green of Epiphany reminds us of everlasting life through Jesus, available even in the cyclical seasons of life and death. Take this opportunity to fill your home with green. Many people force bulbs: Paperwhites or Amaryllis bulbs work great and can be easily found. Stars are the traditional symbols of Epiphany, because the Wise Men followed a star to Jesus. Consider decorating with stars or letting the children create stars and spread them around the house.

It has long been a tradition to ask God to bless our homes during Epiphany. In keeping with the theme of "showing" we are asking God to show up in each room of our homes, and in each person who lives in that room.

Bless The House

A great day to do this is on Epiphany, January 6th. You'll need some candles or flash lights for your "not-so-fire-ready" members, and this simple blessing ritual.

» Turn off all the lights in the house.

» Invite all of the members to gather in a central location. (The kitchen or living room is a good spot.)

» Light candles and give each family member a candle. The smaller members who are not ready for fire responsibilities can be given a flashlight.

» Move together into the nearest room.

» Pray for the people who use that room. If you have never blessed a person before, it is a marvelously powerful action full of grace and love.

» Continue to move through each room in the house, blessing the people who will use it.

» End where you started. Some families conclude this time of blessing with a song, some conclude with prayer, or Scripture reading. My family (Lacy) concludes with cookies. Do what works for you and your people.

How To Bless a Person

Blessings hold a lot of weight in the Scriptures, and because of that we think they are difficult and out of our grasp to give. Not so. Here are a few guidelines for blessings:

» Touch the person you are blessing.

» Speak their name, mentally attaching value to them.

» Tell of the wonderful things that this year will include for them.

» Be willing to help bring the wonderful things to pass.

A blessing might go something like this: Reaching over and touching my daughter on the head, I'd say,

> "Aidan, you are a special child of God. He loves you so much. In this room you study and play. God has given you a spectacular mind and I know that you will do well in Math this year. You will continue to grow in piano and violin; God's gifts live in you. You will also become more patient and loving with your sister who also lives in this room. You will become more like Jesus each day. We your parents promise to help you. Let it be!"

If you would like more information on blessings within the family, John Trent and Gary Smalley have a very insightful book called *The Blessing*.[1]

---

1 John Trent and Gary Smalley, *The Blessing*. Thomas Nelson. 1986.

About the Readings

We read from two different Gospels in this season, as these stretches of Ordinary Time are used to read straight through the Gospels. This is especially important for older children, who can begin to follow the thread of Jesus' ministry as it unfolds. Younger kids, too, will get to know Jesus and see what life in his Kingdom is like as they hear the Gospel read in sequence. During the first week of Epiphany, our readings focus on the miracles of Jesus as recorded in the Gospel of John. After the Last Supper, Jesus tells his disciples that if they can't believe in him just based on his character, they should at least believe because of the works he did. The miracles Jesus performs are one way he "shows" that He is God with us. Then, for the rest of this season, we dive into the Gospel of Mark!

Interestingly, the Gospel readings in Ordinary Time stop short of the events of Holy Week—Palm Sunday, the Crucifixion, and the Resurrection. These are read in full during Holy Week itself. Some people might think this is odd: don't we want to go straight to the Cross, as often and soon as possible? Absolutely, the center and crown of the Gospel is at the Cross and the Empty Tomb. But the purpose here is to keep us from forgetting the rest of the Gospel—what the Cross and Empty Tomb make available! Life with God, in his Kingdom, today! We are looking together at how Jesus lived, what He taught, and discovering what the Gospel says for today, life now.

Because the season of Lent/Easter moves around the calendar each year, Epiphany varies in length. (Don't worry, we've included a calendar in the back so you know when to stop!) For those years when Epiphany is especially long, we finish up by reading the Sermon on the Mount. This is an especially vivid image of life in the Kingdom, and central for our lives as Christians. Be sure to give kids time to ponder the images of a life ruled by agape love.

WEEK OF EPIPHANY

....

Epiphany (January 6)

....

Seasonal Fun:

» **Finish the Christmas story:** This is the day we celebrate the Magi coming to see Jesus. Finally we can move the Magi to the Nativity. If you have already put your Nativity scene away invite the kids to draw pictures of the Magi, or make Magi sculptures. A recipe for homemade clay follow, but also clay can be found in any arts and crafts store. Use old buttons and beads for decorations.

To make clay, mix the ingredients together and cook over low heat until mixture is thick like mashed potatoes. Then dump it onto wax paper until it is cool to the touch, then sculpt.

» 1 cup salt

» 1 cup water

» 1 cup flour

» Food coloring, optional

» **Have a party:** Epiphany also symbolizes that Jesus not only came for the Jewish people but for the whole world. The Magi were not Jewish. The Kingdom of God is for all nationalities and this is the day to celebrate it.

» **Make a King Cake:** There are various forms of this tradition. One way to make a King Cake includes baking a tiny plastic baby into a cake. Really any kind of cake will do. Traditionally the cake is covered in gold and purple frosting or sprinkles to signify royalty. While eating the cake the person who finds the baby gets to wear a crown and be the King of the house for a day. I (Lacy) live in a home with medical personnel so we don't do that one for fear of accidental ingestion of a plastic baby Jesus. (Eating his body in Holy Communion is one thing, but this is entirely another matter.) As a substitution we use a dried bean. We make the cake, but instead of a baby Jesus we use a bean. The person who gets the bean in their piece of cake is the King and wears the paper crown.

» **Hunt for Jesus:** Hide a baby doll wrapped in swaddling clothes in the house. Go through your closet and collect robes, scarves, and anything fancy, and make paper crowns. Invite the children to dress up like kings. Tell them that they are the Magi looking for baby Jesus. Read Matthew 2:1-7 to the children before they embark on their journey; encourage them to use their imaginations. This is extra fun for children if the adults dress up too.

Till: Jesus, thank you for loving all people. You love people from this country, and far away countries, and white people, and brown people, and rich people and poor people and young people and old people—all people. Help us to love all people too.

Plant: Matthew 12:14-21.

Water:

» Imagine it: Imagine what it would be like to see Jesus heal someone. What would you do if he healed you?

» Apply it: The scriptures say Jesus won't yell and he won't walk over anyone's feelings. Jesus knew that words can heal or hurt. How can you use your words today to heal and not hurt?

Weed: Name a time today when words were used to hurt. Maybe you spoke the words; maybe they were spoken to you. Name a time today when words were used to heal. Maybe you spoke the words; maybe they were spoken to you.

Use the following devotions during the days from Epiphany, January 6th, through the following Saturday. For example, if Epiphany falls on Sunday you will need all six days of devotions to get to the next Saturday. If Epiphany falls on Thursday you will need only two days.

Day One

Till: Thank you Jesus for helping us believe in you. Show us today how you are God's Son.

Plant: John 2:1-11

Water:

> » Play it: Invite children to act out the scene in today's Scripture.

> » Live it: Where can you look for God's miracles today?

Weed: Where did you see God's miracles today? Is there a time when you wonder about Jesus being God's Son? Pray and ask God to help you to know the truth.

Day Two

Till: Jesus, you are the miracle maker. Thank you for helping us to believe by giving us miracles. Help us to see your miracles today.

Plant: John 4:46-54

Water:

> » Apply it: Think of someone you know who is sick. Pray for them.

> » Live it: As you go through your day today, watch for people who need Jesus' help and pray for them right then. Shoot silent arrows of prayer at people today.

Weed: Were you able to pray for people today? What was it like to ask Jesus to help people?

Day Three

Till: Jesus, thank you for making us well. Help us want to be well today. We want to be whole people. We want to help others to be whole.

Plant: John 5:1-15

Water:

> » Play it: Invite the children to act out today's scripture drama.

> » Imagine it: Imagine Jesus asking you, "Do you want to be well?" What would you say? Are there some places in your body or your heart that need to be healed?

Weed: How can a person know if their heart needs to be healed? (Pain in the body means the body needs to be healed. It's the same with the heart.) Pray together as a family for someone who needs healing. Ask Jesus to show himself to them.

Day Four

Till: Thank you Jesus for stretching our faith. Help us to see where you are at work today.

Plant: John 6:1-14

Water:

> » Imagine it: Imagine you are the little boy. How would you feel about Jesus using your lunch? What can you, as you are now, give to Jesus to help him make miracles?

> » Apply it: Talk about an event coming up that you think is going to stretch your faith. Invite the family to pray with you about that thing.

Weed: What happened today to stretch your faith? Did your faith grow? Did you help Jesus with miracles today?

Day Five

Till: Thank you God for feeding us. You not only feed our bodies, but you feed our hearts too. Help us to remember that you are the food that lasts forever.

Plant: John 6:15-27

Water:

> » Apply it: What are the things you need for today? Was Jesus a part of your list?

> » Watch it: As you go through your day make a list of things that will last forever.

Weed: How did you need Jesus today? What things made it to your list? Everything decomposes, only God and people last forever. If only God and people last forever, how should we spend our time and money?

Day Six
· · · · · · ·

Till: Jesus, thank you for bringing light into the world. Thank you for helping us to see God and follow him. Help us to look for what God can do.

Plant: John 9:1-12

Water:

> » Play it: Act out today's Scripture.

> » Apply it: Look for the light of Jesus today. How can you bring the light of Jesus where you are?

Weed: Where did you see the light of Jesus today? Where did you bring the light of Jesus today?

EPIPHANY, WEEK 1

....

Light of the World: *North America*

The North American continent is home to 23 countries.[2] If you have a globe or map locate these countries. Choose a different country each day of this week to pray for by name. Consider replacing TV time this week with time learning about one or more of these countries.[3]

In Guatemala children do not receive their gifts on Christmas Day like in the United States and Canada. On January 5th before they go to bed, they fill their shoes with hay. The hay is for the camels of the Magi who come this night in search of the Christ Child. In return the children wake to find gifts in their shoes and the hay is gone. How can you incorporate this tradition into your Epiphany celebrations?

> » Pray for this continent: Father always with us, may your light grow in North America. Help North Americans to seek your face and love their neighbors. Amen.

---

2 Antigua and Barbuda, Bahamas, Barbados, Belize, Canada, Costa Rica, Cuba, Dominica, Dominican Republic, El Salvador, Grenada, Guatemala, Haiti, Honduras, Jamaica, Mexico, Nicaragua, Panama, Saint Kitts and Nevis, Saint Lucia, Saint Vincent and the Grenadines, Trinidad and Tobago, United States.
3 National Geographic's web site is full of information and it's fun: http://www.nationalgeographic.com/kids-world-atlas/

Journaling

The Gospel of Mark lets the main thing be the main thing. No foo-foo details or attempts to make the reader feel like they were there, no appeals to a specific audience—Mark is concise and fact filled. The very best of what you need to know to live a life following Jesus is found in Mark. It's the gospel straight up—hold the olives and ice.

For the next six weeks the Monday through Saturday readings will be in Mark, which is quick and concise. In order to dig deep, we suggest drawing as a meditation. Everyone needs a blank journal; you can share a family collection of colored pencils or crayons. Drawing the scriptures has an amazing ability to draw us into meditating on them. Leap into the scriptures through drawing. Resist the urge to clean up the supper dishes, or check emails while the kids draw. At the very least, you will have given your children an example they can follow.

Each of the six days will have the opportunity for a drawing, so over the course of six weeks, you will have a collection of thirty-six drawings. These drawings will help kids to reflect what Mark has to teach us about Jesus. So hang on to your hat and get ready for the most direct and straight-shooting account of the life of Christ.

Sunday
. . . .

Till: Thank you Jesus that you are the Word of God to us. Thank you that you have always been and always will be. Help us to see your life-light today.

Plant: John 1:1–7, 19–20, 29–34.

Water:

> » Draw it: Date the first journal page, then draw what the Word looks like to you.

> » Apply it: How can you show others the way to the Light today? (Hint: kindness, gentleness, patience, etc. are ways to show the light.)

Weed: Where did you see the Light of Jesus today? When did you show others the Light?

Monday

Till: It's a miracle! The Holy Spirit changes us from the inside out. Thank you for letting us trade in our old life of selfishness and anger for a new life of loving and forgiving others. Jesus, thank you for showing us what God is like.

Plant: Mark 1:1-13

Water:

> » Draw it: Date the page, then listen closely to the reading and draw what it looked like for God to split the sky open.

> » Apply it: John the Baptizer made the way straight for Jesus by helping people to confess their sins to God and commit to walking with God. How do you need to make the way straight today?

Weed: When did you see God today? How did you make the way straight today? If you didn't, do you need to do it now?

Tuesday

Till: "Come with me." You call all of us to come with you. Help us to answer, "Yes, I will come."

Plant: Mark 1:14-28

Water:

> » Draw it: Date the page, then draw what it looked like for the fishermen to drop their nets and follow Jesus.

» Apply it: Brainstorm a list of the things the fishermen had to give up to follow Jesus. What do you need to give up today to follow Jesus?

Weed: When did you hear Jesus ask you, "Come with me." What did you give up today to follow Jesus (such as getting your way, anger, etc.)?

Wednesday

Till: When you were here on earth you cared so much for the sick that you healed them. Thank you for showing us how to care for others. Help us to be full of care for those around us.

Plant: Mark 1:29-45

Water:

» Draw it: Date the page, then choose one of the healings from today's Scripture and draw it.

» Apply it: How can you show care to others today?

Weed: Who did you see today that needed to be cared for? Who did you show care to today?

Thursday

Till: Jesus, you can heal our bodies and our hearts. Help us to ask you not only to heal our bodies, but also to heal our hearts. Thank you for being the great healer.

Plant: Mark 2:1-12

Water:

> » Draw it: Date the page, then draw the friends lowering the man down in front of Jesus.

> » Apply it: What part of you, your heart or your body, needs healing today? Pray with those around you for healing.

Weed: Again, what part of you, your heart or your body, needs healing today? Pray with those around you for healing. Who did you see today that needs healing? Pray for that person.

Friday
. . . . . .

Till: You bring us a new life. Help us to leave our old life behind and want to be like you, to live in your Kingdom.

Plant: Mark 2:13-22

Water:

> » Draw it: Date the page, then draw what it would look like to pour wine into cracked bottles.

> » Apply it: Jesus says that when we're with him, it's time to celebrate that he has come to us. Plan a party for this week. Invite someone who looks like they need a party.

Weed: Discuss the plans for your party. Who should you invite? How is Jesus like the wine, and you like the bottle?

Saturday
. . . .

Till: Jesus, you are in charge. You make the rules. You choose to do good; help us to choose to do good.

Plant: Mark 2:23-3:6

Water:

» Draw it: Date the page, then listen closely to the Scripture being read. What picture stands out in your mind? Draw it. Invite the other family members to guess what you drew, then tell them why you chose it.

» Apply it: Jesus gave people what they needed most. He didn't always give them what they wanted but he gave them what was best for them. Talk about a time you got what you needed, not what you wanted.

Weed: What did you need today? Did you get it? What did you want today? Did you get it?

EPIPHANY, WEEK 2

....

Light of the World: *South America*

The South American continent is home to 12 countries.[4] If you have a globe or map locate these countries. Choose a different country each day of this week to pray for by name. Consider replacing TV time this week with time learning about one or more of these countries.

In Paraguay Epiphany is a celebration complete with parties for children, plays that tell the story of the Magi looking for Jesus, and caroling door to door singing traditional songs about Jesus. How can you incorporate one or more of these traditions into your Epiphany celebration? How can you bring the light of Jesus to your neighborhood through celebration?

» Pray for this continent: Father always with us, may your light grow in South America. Help South Americans to seek your face and love their neighbors. Amen.

Sunday
. . . . . .

Till: Thank you Jesus for showing yourself to all people. Help us to respond like the Samaritan people and follow you.

---

4 Argentina, Bolivia, Brazil, Chile, Colombia, Ecuador, Guyana, Paraguay, Peru, Suriname, Uruguay, Venezuela.

Plant: John 4:27-42.

Water:

» Draw it: Date the page, and draw ripe fields.

» Apply it: In today's reading we find two positive actions: Jesus' action of "eating" the will of God and the Samaritans' action of committing themselves to Jesus. Which action do you need to take today? What would it look like to eat the will of God?

Weed: Which action did you choose to take today? Why and how did you take it?

Monday

Till: Thank you Jesus for passing on God's message of love to the disciples. They passed the message on to others, and then the message was passed on to us. Help us to continue as those before us and pass on the message of God's love to the world today.

Plant: Mark 3:7-19

Water:

» Draw it: Date the page, then draw Jesus on the mountain with his disciples.

» Apply it: How can you pass on the message of God's love today?

» Imagine it: How would you have felt if Jesus had chosen you to be one of his disciples?

Weed: How did you pass on the message of God's love today? How were you one of Jesus disciples today? When did you spend quiet, alone, private time with Jesus today?

Tuesday

Till: We are in God's family. Jesus, it's hard for us to believe that we are in your family, but we are! Thank you God for adopting us! Grow the truth that we belong to you in our hearts and minds.

Plant: Mark 3:20-35

Water:

>> Draw it: Date the page, then draw the family of God and include yourself.

>> Apply it: How can you obey God today?

>> Live it: Look around at the people you are with; they are also in God's family. How can you pray for each other today?

Weed: How did you obey God today? How did it feel to know you were prayed for today?

Wednesday

Till: Thank you Jesus for helping us to understand the Kingdom of God. Help us to know how it works and help us to know how to live there.

Plant: Mark 4:1-20

Water:

>> Draw it: Date the page. Which story about the seed is about you? Which story do you want to be? Draw it.

>> Apply it: How can you hear the word of God and embrace it today?

Weed: Think of your day: which story of the seed were you? How did you embrace the word of God today?

Thursday

Till: Thank you Jesus for using stories to teach us. Sew the truth of the story into the fabric of our hearts and minds. Help us to be like you.

Plant: Mark 4:21-34

Water:

» Draw it: Date the page, then choose one of the illustrations of Kingdom life and draw it.

» Apply it: Jesus says that in God's kingdom giving is more important than getting. What is one way you can give instead of get today?

Weed: What did you give today? How did you live in God's kingdom today?

Friday

Till: Thank you Jesus for always protecting us. Help us to understand that when we are with you, we have nothing to fear.

Plant: Mark 4:35-41

Water:

» Draw it: Date the page, then draw this scene.

» Act it: Act out the scene, using toilet paper as the wind and waves.

Apply it: Is there a storm coming up today or this week? How can you stick close to Jesus?

Weed: How did you stick close to Jesus today? Pray together for guidance in the storms that are coming up.

Saturday
· · · · · · · · · ·

Till: Jesus you are our healer and protector. You heal us and protect us from evil. Help us to tell our stories to others so they can know you, too.

Plant: Mark 5:1-20

Water:

> » Draw it: Date the page, then draw your favorite scene in this story.

> » Live it: Tell about a time Jesus healed or protected you. Share that story with someone this week.

Weed: Where did Jesus heal you or protect you today? Whom did you share your story with? How did it go?

EPIPHANY, WEEK 3

Light of the World: *Africa*

The African continent is home to 54 countries.[5] If you have a globe or map locate these countries. Choose a different country each day of this week to pray for by name. Consider replacing TV time this week with time learning about one or more of these countries.

In Egypt, Coptic Orthodox Christians celebrate and remember the Trinity through the baptism of Jesus. While Jesus was being baptized in the Jordan River, we hear the Father and see the Spirit. We see a joyous Triune God! They love and enjoy each other; and we get a glimpse of it at Jesus' baptism. To commemorate this occasion, Egyptian Coptic Christians participate in a service of blessing water. Then that water is taken to their homes, where the homes are blessed as places where human beings live with God. How can this tradition help you to celebrate Epiphany?

» Pray for this continent: Father always with us, may your light grow in Africa. Help Africans to seek your face and love their neighbors. Amen.

---

5 Algeria, Angola, Benin, Botswana, Burkina, Burundi, Cameroon, Cape Verde, Central African Republic, Chad, Comoros, Congo, Congo, Democratic Republic of, Djibouti, Egypt, Equatorial Guinea, Eritrea, Ethiopia, Gabon, Gambia, Ghana, Guinea, Guinea-Bissau, Ivory Coast, Kenya, Lesotho, Liberia, Libya, Madagascar, Malawi, Mali, Mauritania, Mauritius, Morocco, Mozambique, Namibia, Niger, Nigeria, Rwanda, Sao Tome and Principe, Senegal, Seychelles, Sierra Leone, Somalia, South Africa, South Sudan, Sudan, Swaziland, Tanzania, Togo, Tunisia, Uganda, Zambia, Zimbabwe.

Sunday
. . . .

Till: Thank you Jesus for helping us remember that you are part of the Trinity. God's Son can heal people and he also makes the rules. Thank you for showing us who you are.

Plant: John 5:2-18

Water:

» Draw it: Date the page, then draw the scene at the pool.

» Imagine it: Think about God, Jesus and the Holy Spirit. They are the Trinity—three persons in one. How do you think they get along? How do you think they love each other? Look for the different persons of the Trinity today in God's protection, the Holy Spirit's guidance, and the love of Jesus.

Weed: Where and when did you see the members of the Trinity? What did they look like?

Monday
. . . .

Till: Jesus you care so much for us! You heal us when we are sick. Help us listen to you and trust you to take care of us. We know you can do anything.

Plant: Mark 5:21-43

Water:

» Draw it: Date the page, then draw the scene when Jesus raises the daughter.

» Live it: Many people were telling the man to give up on Jesus since his daughter was dead the situation was hopeless. But Jesus tells the man, "Don't listen to them, just to me." Who is Jesus telling you to ignore? How can you listen more closely to Jesus?

Weed: Whom did you listen to today? When did you hear Jesus and trust him?

Tuesday

Till: Our lives really can be different! Thank you Jesus for showing us new life! Help us to release our stubbornness and follow you. We can trust you for a new way of living.

Plant: Mark 6:1-13

Water:

> » Draw it: Date the page, then really dig deep in your imagination and draw one example of what it would look like to truly trust Jesus today.

> » Apply it: In what ways are you stubbornly against submitting to the radically different life of Jesus? Watch for your stubborn ways and ask Jesus for help every time you see them today.

Weed: How did you live a radically different life today? How did you trust Jesus today? When did you remember to pray?

Wednesday

Till: John had great courage! He had the courage to speak the truth to Herod, even when his life was in danger. Please God, give us the courage to speak the truth when you nudge us to.

Plant: Mark 6:13-29

Water:

> » Draw it: Date the page, then draw John's disciples burying him. Think about the courage he had to speak the truth.

» Play it: Role-play a situation where courage is need to speak the truth (like confessing or refusing to do something wrong even when powerful friends are doing it).

Weed: When did you need courage today? Did you pray? What happened? Name a situation coming up where you will need courage, then pray with your family about it.

Thursday

Till: Jesus you are our shepherd. We are your sheep! You feed us and protect us. Help us to listen to your voice and follow your ways.

Plant: Mark 6:30-46

Water:

» Draw it: Date the page, then draw your favorite image from today's reading.

» Imagine it: Imagine you are one of the disciples and Jesus has just asked you to make dinner for thousands of people. How do you feel? What will you do?

» Apply it: Math in the Kingdom of Heaven is different than the math we know. When we add Jesus to any of our problems, the answer is more than we can imagine. What problem do you have this week that you can add Jesus to?

Weed: What problems did you encounter today? How did you add Jesus to those problems?

Friday

Till: Jesus, the storms in our lives are calmed by you. Help us to really know who you are—not a ghost, not just a story, not just a man. You are God's own Son who loves us. Help us to find comfort in you.

Plant: Mark 6:47-56

Water:

> » Draw it: Date the page, then draw the scene from today's reading, paying close attention to looks on the disciples' faces.

> » Apply it: Is there a storm in your life that you just shake your head at, not knowing why it is or what to do? Invite Jesus into your boat. Let him comfort you and calm the storm in your heart.

> » Imagine it: Imagine you are one of the disciples. You are in a huge storm and suddenly you see a man walk on the water. Quick—how do you react?

Weed: Sometimes our actions cause storms in our hearts that need calming. If we've wronged someone, we can say we're sorry. If we are confused, we can ask for help. If we are lonely, we can be loved. What are the storms in your heart? How can Jesus help your storms? How can your family help your storms?

Saturday

Till: Thank you Jesus for teaching us that our actions come from our heart. Please change our hearts. Help our hearts to be like yours, so our actions will be like yours too.

Plant: Mark 7:1-23

Water:

> » Draw it: Date the page, then draw how our hearts change first, then our actions change.

» List it: Make a list of ways to clean the outside of us (such as obeying our parents, not cheating in school, and living by the Ten Commandments); then make another list of ways to clean the inside of us (such as confessing when we're wrong, talking to Jesus daily, and serving others). When we work to clean the inside, the outside will follow.

Weed: When did you clean the inside today? What did you do to clean the inside today?

EPIPHANY, WEEK 4

. . . .

Light of the World: *Europe*

The European continent is home to 47 countries.[6] If you have a globe or map locate these countries. Choose a different country each day of this week to pray for by name. Consider replacing TV time this week with time learning about one or more of these countries.

In Germany, Epiphany tradition includes children going door to door singing with lanterns in hand that represent the light of Jesus. After singing the children are given pastries or candy. In more modern times the tradition has changed somewhat in that now children go door to door singing, but they collect donations for the poor. How can you incorporate this tradition into your Epiphany celebration?

> » Pray for this continent: Father always with us, may your light grow in Europe. Help Europeans to seek your face and love their neighbors. Amen.

---

6 Albania, Andorra, Armenia, Austria, Azerbaijan, Belarus, Belgium, Bosnia and Herzegovina, Bulgaria, Croatia, Cyprus, Czech Republic, Denmark, Estonia, Finland, France, Georgia, Germany, Greece, Hungary, Iceland, Ireland, Italy, Latvia, Liechtenstein, Lithuania, Luxembourg, Macedonia, Malta, Moldova, Monaco, Montenegro, Netherlands, Norway, Poland, Portugal, Romania, San Marino, Serbia, Slovakia, Slovenia, Spain, Sweden, Switzerland, Ukraine, United Kingdom, Vatican City.

Sunday

Till: Jesus, you taught us that why we act is important. Forgive us and transform us into persons that do good for the right reasons.

Plant: John 7:14-31.

Water:

» Draw it: Date the page, then draw Jesus standing on the temple steps teaching about the heart.

» Think it: Think about the last time you did something good. Did you do good to help others or to make yourself look good?

» Apply it: Ask Jesus to help you to do good today for the good of others.

Weed: When did you do good today? How did you do good for others? Was there a time that you did good to make yourself look good?

Monday

Till: Jesus you are good! You helped people and loved people long ago. And even today you help us and love us. Help us to do good, in the same manner that you did good, for others.

Plant: Mark 7:24-37

Water:

» Draw it: Date the page, then draw the scene where Jesus heals the man who could not speak or hear.

» Play it: Act it out. Choose one of the healings from today's reading and role play.

Weed: When did you see good today? Was Jesus involved? When did you do good today—did you do it for others?

Tuesday

Till: Thank you Jesus for the miracles of your Kingdom! You feed us and you feed thousands of people. Help us to remember that with you anything is possible!

Plant: Mark 8:1-10

Water:

» Draw it: Date the page, then draw Jesus feeding the people.

» Apply it: What are some things you have to do that seem impossible? Add Jesus—ask him to help with the impossible.

Weed: What things were impossible today? Did you add Jesus? What happened?

Wednesday

Till: Jesus you are so patient with us. You teach us over and over again, helping us to understand what is important. Help us to listen and learn.

Plant: Mark 8:11-26

Water:

» Draw it: Date the page, then draw your favorite scene from today's readings.

» Apply it: What is distracting you from hearing Jesus? What can you do about it?

Weed: What kept you from hearing and obeying Jesus today? What did you do about it?

Thursday
. . . .

Till: Thank you Jesus for showing us how to live in the Kingdom by sacrificing yourself. Help us to follow you and not give into our "me-first" thinking.

Plant: Mark 8:27-9:1

Water:

» Draw it: Date the page, then draw Jesus telling Peter about the Kingdom of God, but putting yourself in Peter's place!

» Imagine it: Imagine what it would look like to let others have their way today. How can you let others have their way?

Weed: How did you follow Jesus by sacrificing today? How did it feel to sacrifice? What can you sacrifice tomorrow?

Friday
. . . . . .

Till: Thank you God for visions of heaven. Give us visions of heaven and help us to bring them into our everyday lives.

Plant: Mark 9:2-13

Water:

» Draw it: Date the page. The scene in today's Scripture reading is called the Transfiguration. Draw it.

» Live it: Have you ever had a vision of heaven? How would seeing heaven change how you act every day?

» Apply it: Ask God to show you what heaven is like. Listen and look for his answer.

Weed: Did you see heaven today? How did you bring your vision of heaven into your day?

Saturday

Till: Anything can happen with you, Jesus! Help us with our doubts, help us to believe!

Plant: Mark 9:14-29

Water:

>» Draw it: Date the page, then draw Jesus healing the boy.

>» Live it: The father tells Jesus about his doubts and Jesus helps him with his unbelief. What are your doubts? Share them with Jesus. Ask him and your family for prayer and help.

Weed: When did you doubt today? Did you remember to ask Jesus to help?

EPIPHANY, WEEK 5

. . . .

Light of the World: *Asia*

The Asian continent is home to 44 countries.[7] If you have a globe or map locate these countries. Choose a different country each day of this week to pray for by name. Consider replacing TV time this week with time learning about one or more of these countries.

In India, Epiphany marks the end of Advent and Christmastide. At home and at church they mark this ending by putting away Nativity scenes and decorations, although this is not a solemn occasion. Indians celebrate the end of the Season with a festive carnival complete with fully costumed Magi, a procession, and a court. How can you incorporate this tradition into your Epiphany celebration?

> » Pray for this continent: Father always with us, may your light grow in Asia. Help Asians to seek your face and love their neighbors. Amen.

---

7 Afghanistan, Bahrain, Bangladesh, Bhutan, Brunei, Burma (Myanmar), Cambodia, China, East Timor, India, Indonesia, Iran, Iraq, Israel, Japan, Jordan, Kazakhstan, Korea, North, Korea, South, Kuwait, Kyrgyzstan, Laos, Lebanon, Malaysia, Maldives, Mongolia, Nepal, Oman, Pakistan, Philippines, Qatar, Russian Federation, Saudi Arabia, Singapore, Sri Lanka, Syria, Tajikistan, Thailand, Turkey, Turkmenistan, United Arab Emirates, Uzbekistan, Vietnam, Yemen.

Sunday

Till: You give us living water! We do thirst, Lord Jesus—we come to you. Give us your living water.

Plant: John 7:37-46.

Water:

» Draw it: Date the page, then draw Jesus as living water.

» Play it: Role play the dialog in today's reading. Pay particular attention to the last line, "Have you heard the way he talks? We've never heard anyone speak like this man."

» Apply it: How is Jesus like living water?

Weed: When did you need the living water of Jesus today? How did your words give life today?

Monday

Till: Thank you Jesus for showing us how to serve others. Help us to follow your example.

Plant: Mark 9:30-41

Water:

» Draw it: Date the page, then draw Jesus with the children.

» Apply it: Jesus told his disciples that those who are first in the kingdom serve others. How can you serve your family today?

Weed: How did you serve your family today? How can you serve others tomorrow?

Tuesday

Till: God, you are devoted to us in every way. Help us to be devoted to you. Forgive us when we are distracted. Help us to make the choice to focus on you.

Plant: Mark 9:42-50

Water:

» Draw it: Date the page, then draw Jesus protecting the childlike believers.

» Apply it: There are many things in life that can distract us from knowing God. Make a list of some things that keep you from knowing God more. Choose one or two and get rid of them. (This is the discipline of simplicity: letting go of things that keep us from God. Richard Foster has written an excellent book on simplicity called *The Freedom of Simplicity*.[8])

Weed: As you reflect on your day, what things kept you from knowing God? What things did you choose to get rid of? How did you do without them?

Wednesday

Till: Yes Jesus, you do love the little children. We are grateful that you protect the children and want the children near you. Thank you for using the little children to teach adults.

Plant: Mark 10:1-16

Water:

» Draw it: Date the page, then draw Jesus with the little children.

» Apply it: Jesus blessed the children. Take the time today to give a special blessing to the children in your household. If you are unsure how

---

8 Richard J. Foster *The Freedom of Simplicity*. HarperCollins. 2010.

to give a blessing, reread the section on blessing in the Epiphany intro-
duction.

» Live it: As you go through your day today, shoot arrows of blessing at
every child you see. Ask God to show you how to have the simplicity
of a child.

Weed: Tell about shooting arrows of blessing at children. How can you have
the simplicity of a child?

Thursday

Till: Thank you Jesus for showing us how your Kingdom works. Those who
have everything, and give up nothing are last in your Kingdom. Great love and
sacrifice are important to you. Help them to be important to us.

Plant: Mark 10:17-31

Water:

» Draw it: Date the page, then draw the rich man and Jesus.

» Apply it: Tie a balloon to the ceiling, just out of reach of the children.
Tell the children that whoever can touch that balloon can get a special
prize. (Be sure and actually have a small prize ready.) Give the children
a chance to try and touch the balloon. When all have failed, lift one
child up to touch the balloon. Tell the children that the Kingdom of
God is like that. We cannot live in God's kingdom without help. It's out
of our reach, and no matter how hard we try, we can't do it by ourselves.
But if we ask for God's help and we let him help us, we can!

Weed: When did you ask for God's help today? When should you have asked
for God's help today?

Friday

Till: God, your ways are different from the way of people. But you know what is best for us. You know us and understand us because you made us. Help us, God, to serve others.

Plant: Mark 10:32-45

Water:

» Draw it: Date the page, then draw Jesus' disciples being afraid.

» Live it: Reread the last paragraph in today's reading. What has the Son of Man come to do? How can you serve others today? How can you choose *not* to get your way?

Weed: Who did you serve today? What was their response when you served them? How did you not get your way today?

Saturday

Till: Son of David, Jesus! Have mercy! Heal us from blindness. Help us see you and others around us.

Plant: Mark 10:46-52

Water:

» Draw it: Date the page, then draw the scene in today's reading.

» Live it: We are also blind. Sometime we don't want to see Jesus in others. Today take the time to look at people in the eyes and smile. Look at the cashier in the grocery store line, look at the lunch lady in the school cafeteria, and look at people you don't normally talk with at school or work. Let others see the light of Jesus in your eyes and your smile.

Weed: Who did you look at and smile at today? How did it feel to spread the light of Jesus with your eyes and your smile?

EPIPHANY, WEEK 6

. . . .

Light of the World: *Oceania*

Oceania is home to 14 countries.[9] If you have a globe or map locate these countries. Choose a different country each day of this week to pray for by name. Consider replacing TV time this week with time learning about one or more of these countries.

In New Zealand, Christians begin Epiphany by announcing the date of Easter. In this way they announce and focus on the most central event in Christian history, the death and resurrection of Jesus. How can you incorporate this tradition into your Epiphany celebration?

> » Pray for this continent: Father always with us, may your light grow in Oceania. Help those who live there to seek your face and love their neighbors. Amen.

Sunday

. . . .

Till: Jesus you are the light of the world. Your light shows us God, our Father. We want to be in the light too, as you are in the light.

---

9 Australia, Fiji, Kiribati, Marshall Islands, Micronesia, Nauru, New Zealand, Palau, Papua New Guinea, Samoa, Solomon Islands, Tonga, Tuvalu, Vanuatu.

Plant: John 8:12-19

Water:

- » Draw it: Date the page, then draw Jesus as the light.

- » Imagine it: Turn all the lights off. Say, "This is what it's like to live our lives without Jesus." Now, light a single candle in the middle of the gathering. Say, "This candle is the light of Jesus. How does Jesus bring light to us? How can we look for his light?"

Weed: Where did you see the light of Jesus today? When did you bring the light of Jesus to others today?

Monday

Till: Hosanna! Blessed are you who comes in the name of the Lord. We worship you Son of God. We want to worship you all day long!

Plant: Mark 11:1-11

Water:

- » Draw it: Date the page, then draw the scene from today's reading.

- » Apply it: Worship begins with thankfulness. Invite everyone to voice their thankful prayer, "Thank you God for_____. You are so good to me." Voice this prayer over and over as thankfulness wells up inside your hearts. When everyone has voiced what is in their hearts, conclude with silent worship or break into song.

Weed: What happened today that you are thankful for? Repeat the "Apply it" section for today.

Tuesday

Till: Jesus, thank you for using so many pictures to teach us. Help us to be good students and to embrace this life in the Kingdom you lived in and talked about so much.

Plant: Mark 11:12-26

Water:

» Draw it: Date the page, then draw a "before and after" picture of the fig tree.

» Apply it: Often when we think of the word "embrace" we think of wrapping our arms around someone and pulling them to us. Grandmothers love to embrace their grandchildren. How can you really embrace this God life today?

Weed: When did you embrace your life in God's kingdom today? When did you ignore your life in God's kingdom?

Wednesday

Till: God, you are patient and good. You have sent messenger after messenger to tell us of your kingdom. Help us to listen to and obey your son, Jesus.

Plant: Mark 11:27-12:12

Water:

» Draw it: Date the page, then choose your favorite scene from today's reading and draw it.

» Play it: Act out the parable Jesus told.

Weed: How was God patient with you today? When or where do you need to listen to Jesus more clearly? How can you do that?

Thursday

Till: You are the living God. You are not a statue, you are not created, you are the Creator. You are eternal—you are God!

Plant: Mark 12:13-27

Water:

» Draw it: Date the page, then draw the scene where the Pharisees ask about taxes.

» Live it: Jesus tell us that people live forever. Humans are eternal beings. Knowing that you will live forever, what are you going to do today to live in God's kingdom?

» Apply it: Look at the people around you today and think of them as people who will live forever.

Weed: How did you live today differently knowing you will live forever? How did you look at people differently, knowing that they will live forever?

Friday

Till: God, you are the one true God—the God of the universe—and there is no other. Help us to follow your commandments to love you and to love others.

Plant: Mark 12:28-34

Water:

» Draw it: Date the page, then draw the two commandments Jesus gives.

» Apply it: How can you show love to God and to others today?

Weed: How did you show love to God today? How did you show love to others today?

Saturday

Till: Jesus, you gave all you had to us. You even gave your life. Help us to give all we have to you. Forgive us when we give you our leftovers.

Plant: Mark 12:35-44

Water:

» Draw it: Date the page, draw the poor widow giving her money.

» Live it: In God's kingdom the math is different than what we know. In God's kingdom when someone gives all they have, no matter how little, it's more than what others give when they only give their leftovers. How can you give all you have to God today?

Weed: What did you give to God today? Did you give all you had or your leftovers?

EPIPHANY, WEEK 7

. . . .

Light of the World: *Antarctica*

There are no countries on Antarctica. However, scientists do live there periodically while they conduct research. Antarctica is home to many varieties of living things, just not human living things. If you have a globe or map locate Antarctica. Consider replacing TV time this week with time learning about Antarctica, its animals, and the scientists who work there.[10]

» Pray for this continent: Father always with us, may your light grow in Antarctica. Help those who work there to seek your face and love their neighbors. Amen.

Introduction to the Sermon on the Mount

Once a famous Christian speaker approached the pulpit and stated seriously: "You are about to hear the best sermon ever preached." The conference-goers shifted uncomfortably in their seats, glancing at one another nervously. What kind of message could follow such a pompous claim? But then the speaker proceeded to read, without comment, Matthew 5–7, Jesus' Sermon on the Mount—and then he sat down!

Sure enough, this is the best sermon we could ask for. It's Jesus' way of painting in vivid colors what life in his Kingdom looks like. Rather than lay-

---

10 http://www.nationalgeographic.com/topics/antarctica/

ing down a bunch of rules, Jesus explodes the idea that external conformity to laws is a good life. Instead, he leads us to the heart—to a transformed inner person that doesn't need to worry, manipulate, condemn or impress. Why not? Because we live in the Kingdom of God, a perfectly good place to be where all our needs are met by our Father who is always with us!

For kids, the biggest idea the Sermon presents is that God is really with us. They may not be able to understand why they choose to tell lies, exaggerate to get their way, or attempt to wheedle and manipulate, but the truth remains: if they can trust that they are safe in God's care, they (like all of us) are far less prone to mess with sin. God's way is just better: happy (blessed!) are those who trust in him, no matter their circumstances!

Sunday
. . . .

Till: Jesus, you are our Shepherd, and you know us each by name! Help us to listen for your voice, and follow you today.

Plant: John 10:7-16.

Water:

> » Enter it: Jesus says that we are his sheep, and that he knows us. What are some things that Jesus knows about you? (Parents, help your children identify good traits, abilities, as well as fears and struggles, but keep the balance toward the positive.) Jesus also says that we will know him. What is Jesus like? (Perhaps kids could glance through the Book of Mark Journal they drew in to spark thoughts.)

> » Apply it: How does it help you today to remember that Jesus knows you inside and out?

Weed: Did anything today spark your memory that Jesus knows you? How did that make you feel? Let's pick something to be a reminder tomorrow that Jesus is our shepherd. (This could be an activity, an object, even the sound of an alarm on a watch.)

Monday

Till: Father, we live the good life because we live with you! Help us remember that, no matter what our circumstances are, we are blessed.

Plant: Matthew 5:1-12

Water:

» Apply it: Today starts our two-week trek through the Sermon on the Mount! Jesus is teaching about the good life—the kind of life that really makes us happy. Today's reading is often called the "Beatitudes" which means "blessings." Jesus is telling us who is happy. But isn't it a strange list? People at the end of their rope, who have lost what is dear to them, who are put down or hurt for loving Jesus... they're the ones Jesus says can be happy! And Jesus is right—because no matter what our circumstances, if God is with us, our life is good! Let's make a modern-day list: who might Jesus call "happy" today, just because God will include them? (Parents, help kids think of people they might not expect to be blessed—the homeless, the poor, the sick, the lonely, etc.)

Weed: Look back on today—were there any hard or painful things that happened? Were you able to remember that God was with you, even then? How could we remind ourselves of God's blessing even in hard times?

Tuesday

Till: God, you make us like salt that adds flavor, like light that brightens up the darkness. Help us to shine your light today, by loving others well and obeying you happily.

Plant: Matthew 5:13-20

Water:

» Play it: Gather as many flashlights, candles, or easily portable lamps as you can into a darkened room. Ask your kids, "What are some ways we can show God's love at home? At school?" For each answer, turn on a light or light a candle. Let the brightness shine!

» Apply it: Jesus says you are the light of the world! Your love and generosity brighten up the lives of others and help them to see God. What is one way you want to shine God's love today? Is there someone hard to love, or something hard to share, that you could try?

Weed: How did your light-shining experiment go? How did you feel when you loved in a new way? How do you think the other person felt when you showed them love?

Wednesday
· · · · · · · · · · · · ·

Till: Jesus, we admit that we get angry and even want to hurt others sometimes. Help us forgive from our hearts, be understanding, and show mercy, just like you do.

Plant: Matthew 5:21-26

Water:

» Enter it: For the next few days, Jesus is helping us understand that what really matters to him is our heart. We might not actually murder a person we're angry with, but in our minds we hate them! Jesus wants us to learn how not to hold a grudge inside, not even to mutter insults under our breath. What are some situations that make you angry with people?

» Apply it: Remember the Beatitudes? Jesus says that in every circumstance, if God is with us, then we are blessed! In the situations you named that make you angry, do you think you need to be angry if God is promising to take care of you? How can you remember this when you feel angry today?

Weed: Did anyone make you angry today? Were you able to remember that God was with you, right then? How can you show forgiveness to that person tomorrow?

Thursday

Till: God, help us to tell the truth, and to love the truth. We don't need to grab control, lie or fool people, because you will make sure we get what we need. Help us trust you today!

Plant: Matthew 5:27-37

Water:

> » Enter it: What are some situations when you are tempted to exaggerate, stretch the truth, or outright lie? Does it seem like using words this way will help you? (Parents, you may want to help kids think about exaggerating stories or bragging to friends. They might not consider this lying, missing the subtlety of manipulative words.)

> » Apply it: Jesus teaches that we don't need to lie. Remember the Beatitudes again! We don't have to get our way in order to be blessed; we just need God. What is one situation today when you can trust God and tell only the truth?

Weed: How did your truth-telling experiment go? How did others react? How did you feel? Was it hard? No matter how it turned out, God was taking care of you and promises always to do so. What is one situation tomorrow that you will need to remember this, so you will tell the truth then?

Friday
......

Till: Jesus, you didn't wait to love us until we cleaned up and impressed you—your love came and found us when we were your enemies! Thank you! Please teach us to love like you do, generously loving the good and the bad alike.

Plant: Matthew 5:38-48

Water:

» Enter it: Jesus is teaching us to be like him, to love even our enemies! Who do you have a hard time loving? How do you think Jesus feels about that person?

» Apply it: Back to the Beatitudes again. If God is really taking care of us, then we've got more than enough blessing to go around. We don't have to hoard our energy just for people we like; we can freely bless anyone, even if they don't deserve it. What is one way you can show kindness to this person you tend to dislike?

Weed: How did your love-your-enemy experiment go today? How did it feel to be kind? How did God provide for you today, even though you gave energy to an "enemy?"

Saturday
....

Till: God, help us to live for your applause, your approval, only. Help us get the reward we really want—you!

Plant: Matthew 6:1-16

Water:

» Apply it: Today, Jesus is teaching us that because it is God whom we really need—not other people's approval—we don't need to act, perform, or pretend to be good to impress others. Let's practice that today by doing an act of secret service! Try not to be caught! Do something nice for someone else—maybe clean up after them when they're not looking, or make something nice for them, or do a chore for them—without telling anyone. Do it so only God sees!

Weed: You don't need to tell what you did (it's a secret!), but how did your act of secret service make you feel?

EPIPHANY, WEEK 8

....

Light of the World: *Adopt a Continent*

We've now covered seven continents. Choose one and go back and take another look at the countries on that continent. Consider "adopting" that continent, educating your family about the countries, their needs, and the move of the Holy Spirit in their midst. Spend this whole year in prayer and continual information gathering. Consider contacting missionaries in these lands, or supporting a child through www.compassion.com or www.worldvision.org.

Sunday
....

Till: Jesus, you are worth everything we have, everything we are! Teach us to worship you extravagantly. We love you!

Plant: John 12:1-8.

Water:

>> Enter it: In today's reading, Mary worships Jesus in an extravagant way—over-the-top, lavish, giving gifts that cost her a lot. She shows that she thinks he is worth everything. Why do you think she does that?

>> Apply it: How can we worship Jesus extravagantly today?

Weed: How did it make you feel to worship Jesus extravagantly? Is there anything you are tempted to pay more attention to than Jesus? Why is he better than those things?

Monday
. . . .

Till: Father who is always with us, let us make a big deal about you! Let things happen your way, because you know best. Give us our everyday needs. Forgive us, help us forgive others. And keep us safe today!

Plant: Matthew 6:7-15

Water:

» Apply it: Jesus teaches us how to talk to God! The good news is that we don't have to get God's attention or trick him into answering us. He's right here, always with us, and cares about our daily needs. Parents, write out on a poster a kid-friendly version of the Lord's Prayer—the version above, or your own paraphrase—and lead your children in praying it throughout this week (at mealtimes, bedtime, etc.).

Weed: When did you talk to God today? What things did you share with him? Was there time when you forgot to include God in your day? How can you include him more tomorrow?

Tuesday
. . . .

Till: Read the Lord's Prayer again.

Plant: Matthew 6:16-23

Water:

» Enter it: What are some things you really like a lot? Do you think about them a lot? Do they wear out, get old, break? What about God?

» Create it: Make a treasure box! For each child, find an empty box (an old shoebox will work). Children can decorate the outside, and will love having their name prominently displayed on the lid. Have your children write down or draw pictures of their favorite truth about God: for example, that God loves them, or that he is preparing a home for them with him in heaven. Have them put these in their treasure box. Keep the treasure box someplace special, and from time to time add in a meaningful verse, or something God does that amazes you. Return to it to remember that God is our treasure!

Weed: How did making your treasure box make you feel about God today? Do you have any "treasure" that you might want to add to the box after today?

Wednesday

Till: Read the Lord's Prayer again.

Plant: Matthew 6:24-34

Water:

» Play it: This activity is silly but celebrates what Jesus is teaching: play the song *Don't Worry, Be Happy* and dance! If we can't dance because God provides all we need, when can we dance? Throughout today, whenever someone feels worried, hum or sing the chorus to this song. (Parents, it is especially instructive to kids if you do this when you are worried. They learn a lot by seeing you dealing with your own brokenness and fear.)

» Apply it: When are you tempted to think you are missing out? How can you remember not to worry, but trust God instead?

Weed: Was there any time today that you felt worried? Did remembering God's love help? How did God provide for you today?

Thursday
. . . .

Till: Read the Lord's Prayer again.

Plant: Matthew 7:1-12

Water:

> » Enter it: Jesus gives us a good way to think about how to treat people: think what you'd want someone to do to you, and do the same for them. Why do you think this is a good idea?

> » Apply it: Look for ways to do for other people what you'd hope they would do for you. But first, let's brainstorm: what are some ways you would like to be treated today? How can you do that for others?

Weed: How was your experiment of treating others like you'd want to be treated? Did you forget and treat anyone in a way you wouldn't want to be treated? Let's ask God's forgiveness, because he is forgiving.

Friday
. . . . . .

Till: Read the Lord's Prayer again.

Plant: Matthew 7:13-21

Water:

> » Create it: In today's reading, Jesus teaches that we can tell a tree by its fruit, because what is on the inside eventually shows up on the outside. Draw two pictures: one, a tree with shiny beautiful fruit; the other, a tree with yucky, rotting fruit.

>   Apply it: Jesus wants to take us and make our lives bear really wonderful fruit! (You could read Ephesians 2:8-10 here, with older children.) What is one area you think God wants to help you grow in during this season? What is a small step you can take today?

Weed: How did your small step go? Was it easy? Hard? What small step can you take tomorrow to grow?

Saturday

Till: Read the Lord's Prayer again.

Plant: Matthew 7:22-29

Water:

>   Play it: Have kids act out the parable of the wise builder and the foolish builder. They can make believe and act the story; or use Legos or Silly Putty to build two houses, one on rock and the other on sand, and then let the storm go crazy!

>   Apply it: Over the last two weeks, we've looked at Jesus' teaching. Now he wraps up by saying that, if we are wise we will put what he says into practice. That means we should be his student, and learn from him how to live well. What is one way you can be Jesus' student today?

Weed: How was it being Jesus' student today? What did you practice that he taught? How can you be Jesus' student tomorrow?

LAST WEEK OF EPIPHANY

Use these last three days to begin the week of Ash Wednesday. To find that date, see the chart in the back of this book. In some years, you will have to cut short your journey through Mark or the Sermon on the Mount, but don't worry: the Gospel readings for those weeks get picked up in the Ordinary Time that comes after Easter. It is the end of Epiphany; now is the time to begin to take down the stars you hung at the start of the season, and prepare for the somber yet joyful waiting of Lent.

Sunday

Till: Jesus, you not only taught but showed us that when we entrust our lives to you and give up everything, we don't lose out. No, our life blossoms forth like a seed into the most beautiful flowers! Help us be reckless with love, laying down our lives as servants.

Plant: John 12:24-32

Water:

» Enter it: This reading takes place just a little before Jesus was crucified. He knows all the pain he was about to suffer for us, but he goes ahead anyway because of how much he loves us and his Father! Then God shouts from heaven, telling Jesus that he is doing the right thing. How do you think Jesus felt when he heard his Father's voice?

» Apply it: Jesus taught that our lives are like seeds: in order to bear fruit, a seed has to look like it's gone for good, lost and buried in the ground! But then it bursts forth into wonderful fruit. Sometimes, in order to love people well, it can look like we have to lose what we need. Are there any ways that God is inviting you to love that look hard or painful? How can you trust God and love in this situation?

Weed: Was there a time today when you had the opportunity to love and it cost you something to do so? How did you do? Was it hard? What happened?

Monday
. . . .

Till: O Jesus, you show us who God really is! Only you could do that, because you are God! You were always, always with God, and then you came right here among us to help us know him. We praise you!

Plant: John 1:1-18

Water:

» Apply it: Epiphany has been a season of Jesus' showing the world what God is really like. What have you learned from Jesus about who God is?

» Play it: Celebrate Jesus! Turn on some loud, fun music and dance while praising God! Spend some time brainstorming how you can make this day a celebration of Jesus' teaching us what God is really like, so we can live with him forever. Then celebrate!

Weed: How was celebrating Jesus? How did our celebration make you feel? What have you learned about God this Epiphany season?

Tuesday

Till: Lord, help us make a straight path for you, right into our hearts! Help us let go of anything that keeps us from loving, worshipping, and following you every day.

Plant: John 1:19-28

Water:

> » Apply it: Tomorrow begins the long season of Lent—forty days of preparation for Easter. Over the years, many Christians have prepared for Easter by entering into some kind of fast. Like the Psalmist in Psalm 63, they wanted to cry out, "My soul hungers for you, O God!" and took steps in order to feel that way. It can be good for children to decide on something to let go of this season to remind them that Jesus is what they really need. Today would be a good day to decide, but approach this carefully with kids. You will want them to feel invited into something that helps them know God better, not forced or punished into losing something they really love. The very youngest children may not understand this distinction, so for them it's probably best to wait until they are older. (For more on family approaches to Lenten fasting, see the next volume of *Good Dirt: Lent, Holy Week & Eastertide,* which available at www.gooddirtfamilies.com)

Weed: What is one way you can prepare your heart today for Jesus tomorrow?

CHURCH YEAR CALENDAR

· ·

Year	Advent	Lent	Holy Week	Easter	Pentecost
2013-14	Dec 1	Mar 5	April 13	April 20	June 8
2014-15	Nov 30	Feb 18	March 29	April 5	May 24
2015-16	Nov 29	Feb 10	March 20	March 27	May 15
2016-17	Nov 27	Mar 1	April 9	April 16	June 4
2017-18	Dec 3	Feb 14	March 25	April 1	May 20
2018-19	Dec 2	Mar 6	April 14	April 21	June 9
2019-20	Dec 1	Feb 26	April 5	April 12	May 31
2020-21	Nov 29	Feb 17	March 28	April 4	May 23
2021-22	Nov 28	Mar 2	April 10	April 17	Jun 5
2022-23	Nov 27	Feb 22	April 2	April 9	May 28
2023-24	Dec 3	Feb 14	March 24	March 31	May 19
2024-25	Dec 1	Mar 5	April 13	April 20	Jun 8
2025-26	Nov 30	Feb 18	March 29	April 5	May 24
2026-27	Nov 29	Feb 10	March 21	March 28	May 16
2027-28	Nov 28	Mar 1	April 9	April 16	Jun 4
2028-29	Dec 3	Feb 14	March 25	April 1	May 27

CONTRIBUTORS

Lacy Finn Borgo

Lacy Finn Borgo writes for the spiritual formation of children because she has children and she likes them. She has a Master's Degree in Education from the State University of New York Geneseo and has taught in both public and private schools in Texas, New York, Colorado, and Kazakhstan. Lacy is a graduate of the Renovaré Institute for Spiritual Formation. She is the author of *Life with God for Children: Engaging Biblical Stories and Practices for Spiritual Formation* released by Renovaré. Lacy has written three picture books—*Big Mama's Baby, Day and Night,* and *The Mighty Hurricane.* Lacy lives in Colorado where she tends both the physical and spiritual gardens of her family.

Ben Barczi

Ben Barczi serves as Pastor of Spiritual Formation at First Baptist Church in San Luis Obispo, CA. He is a graduate of California Polytechnic in San Luis Obispo, where he studied Philosophy, and a graduate of the Renovaré Institute for Spiritual Formation. Ben loves teaching about spiritual formation, and enjoys living a semi-monastic life ordered by the rhythms of Daily Prayer, regular solitude, and lots of really good conversations at amazing local coffeeshops.